STORYTELLING AT WORK

How Moments of Truth on the Job Reveal the Real Business of Life

Mitch Ditkoff

ADVANCED PRAISE

"I truly LOVE this book! The last time I read anything this good was Robert Fulghum's All I Really Need to Know I Learned in Kindergarten, *and that was 25 years ago! With* Storytelling at Work, *Mitch Ditkoff has delivered a modern classic on how to communicate with wisdom. Kudos!"*

—Rowan Gibson, author of *The Four Lenses of Innovation*

"Through storytelling that is both enlightened and primal, this collection whispers our humanity with a soaringly purposeful fresh new voice. Each tale is dipped in optimism balanced with inspired guidance that raises a leader's heart and reminds us of what is indeed possible. The stories transport us and transform our understanding of the deep meaning that lies just below the surface. If wit and wisdom had a love child, they would name him Mitch Ditkoff."

—Doug Stuke, Director,
Aetna Consumer Business Learning and Performance

"I suggest you read Storytelling at Work *with a pencil so you can record the great story ideas that will pop into your mind. Storytelling requires rituals of story finding. Because Mitch offers his own true stories with application ideas that answer, 'So what?' and 'Now what?' your mind is magically compelled to reciprocate with your own story and application ideas that will speak your truth, in your style, to achieve your goals."*

—Annette Simmons, author of *Whoever Tells the Best Idea Wins*

"*Mitch's storytelling reminds us that the truth is rarely in the bottom right corner of an Excel spreadsheet. It's already inside of us.*"

—Jon Bidwell, Chief Innovation Officer, Chubb Insurance

"*Mitch Ditkoff is a master storyteller, weaving tales that not only draw you in, but invite you to see the world with wider eyes. This gem of a book lovingly inspires us to step a little more bravely outside our box.*"

—Susan Stiffleman, author of *Parenting with Presence*

"*If you are a business leader committed to creating a humane, inspired, learning organization, Storytelling at Work is for you.*"

—Chuck Frey, author, *Mindmapping Software Blog*

"*Storytelling at Work is filled with Eureka moments that will spark your creativity and ignite your motivation. Mitch Ditkoff has a magical ability to elevate the routine work of everyday life. Original and deeply insightful!*"

—Marshall Goldsmith, author of *Triggers*, a *New York Times* and *Wall Street Journal* #1 Best Seller

"*Mitch Ditkoff's powerfully written book shows us how storytelling, well done, humanizes the world of work. But even more than that, it helps us pause, go beyond convention, and tune into the deep well of timeless wisdom within.*"

—Tim Gallwey, author of *The Inner Game of Tennis*

To Prem Rawat,
who has shown me what exists beyond story.

"*Work is love made visible. And if you cannot work with love, but only with distaste, it is better that you should leave your work and sit at the gate of the temple and take alms of those who work with joy.*"

—Khalil Gibran

"*It's not what you look at that matters. It's what you see.*"

—Henry David Thoreau

"*I don't like work... but I like what is in work – the chance to find yourself. Your own reality – for yourself, not for others – which no other man can ever know.*"

—Joseph Conrad

"*The moment one gives close attention to anything, even a blade of grass, it becomes a mysterious, awesome, indescribably magnificent world in itself.*"

—Henry Miller

ACKNOWLEDGMENTS

A big thank you to all the wonderful people who supported my GoFundMe campaign:

Claudia Watts • Dave Watts • Steven Greene • Stuart Hoffman
Ron Brent • Joan Apter • Fernando Garcia Munoz • Joe Belinsky
Claudia Hirsch • Craig Klawuhn • Fabio Rangel • Jim Burns
Elliot Landy • Mary Ann Heenehan • Kathy Willis • Eve Baer
Michelle Cameron • Peter Weeks • Johan Drejare • Chris Corbett
Allen Feld • Peter Vowels • Suzee Kaanoi • Allen Imbarrato
Tom Muir • Lori Schweitzer-Amato • Paul Kwicienski • Eve Roha
Barry Ollman • Sarah Jacob • Denny Snyder • Janie Upham
Anna Carney Melcher • Sharon Gilbert • Srima Wijekoon
Melissa Gibson, and Terry Mandolfo

And a big thank you to all the folks who gave me feedback and encouragement:

Evelyne Pouget • Jesse Ditkoff • Mimi Ditkoff • Catharine Clarke
Chris Hamerton • Ginger Haffney • Sharon Jeffers • Joe Belinsky
Gary Ockenden • Lisa Knudsen • Jon Bidwell • Mike Frick
Val Vadeboncoeur • Scott Cronin • Nettie Reynolds
Micah Blumenthal • Mary Jane Fahey • Carl Frankel
Annette Simmons • Premlata Hudson Rawat • Lynn Kindler
Cassandra Mitchell • Tim Gallwey • Prentiss Uchida • Aaron Barr
Alan Jones • Alaya Love • Aliza Corrado • Mark Appleman
Noel Phillips • Stuart Hoffman • Bill Salmansohn
Paul Solis Cohen • Maria DeFranco • Jennifer Edwards
Cary Bayer • Nathan Brenowitz • Laurie Schwartz • Doug Stuke
Ellen Goldberg • Seth Godin • Fuzzbee Morse • Lucas Handwerker
Caleb Rudge • Ilfra Halley • Steve Ornstein • Steven McHugh
Jess Seilheimer • Carl Sorvino • Nancy Seroka • Jennifer Flaherty
Jody Johnson • Barbara Bash • Steve Gorn • Caroline Richey
Steve Kowarsky • Jonathan Lloyd • Julian West • Jule Kowarsky
Jan Buchalter • Larry Lustbader • Marc Black • Rowan Gibson
Marshall Goldsmith • Chuck Frey • Lynnea Brinkerhoff
Michael Margolies • Judith Hyde • Richard Erickson
Melissa Eppard • Suresh Schlanger • Jack Vincent
Monika Winslow • Erika Andersen • Susan Stiffleman
Alan Cohen • Gil Hanson, and Norm Magnuson.

TABLE OF CONTENTS

PART TWO: The Art and Science of Storytelling

THE TIMELESS POWER OF STORY

"The universe is not made of atoms. It is made of stories."
—Muriel Rukeyser

Once upon a time, there was a wealthy merchant traveling across India on a month-long business trip. Two days into his journey, he was befriended by a young man who seemed so gracious and dutiful that the merchant hired him, on the spot, to be his valet for the remainder of the journey. Each night the two of them dined together on the finest of foods and each night the young man excused himself to search the merchant's room, looking for money to steal. He found nothing. On the final night of the journey, racked with guilt, the thief confessed.

"Kind sir, ever since we met I have had only one thing in mind – to rob you. Each night I searched your room, looking under your pillow and everywhere else, but I never found a penny. Your kindness has humbled me and now all I can do is ask your forgiveness. But before we go our separate ways, I must ask one thing: *Where in the world did you hide your money?*"

"Ah…" replied the merchant. "I knew from the moment we met that you were a thief. So I hid my money in the only place I knew you wouldn't look – under *your* pillow."

This book is about the riches under *your* pillow – not only while you're travelling across India, *but also while you're at work.* The riches? Wisdom. The pillow? Stories where your wisdom is hiding.

The FedEx logo is a perfect, modern-day example of this phenomenon.

Most people see only letters, colors, or the word itself. They rarely see *the white arrow* in between the second "E" and the "x." (Next time you see a FedEx logo, look for it). The arrow has *always* been there, but only a small percentage of people ever notice it.

Just like the FedEx logo and the place under our pillows, there are hidden treasures for each of us at work. Not data. Not information. Not even knowledge. *Wisdom.* Yes, *wisdom* – the depth of human understanding not subject to news cycles, social media, or the latest business fad.

Why does connecting with our stories and the wisdom hidden within them matter? Because our stories offer us essential clarity, insight, and understanding.

We don't need *more* technology to find our wisdom. We don't need a Ph.D. We don't need to go on a pilgrimage. We need the willingness to decode what's going on beneath the surface of our lives – those recollections, hidden in our stories, of memorable moments of truth that have happened to us.

Most of us don't take the time to recollect and reflect. Ruled by the routine, we miss the extraordinary. Distracted by the short-term, we miss the timeless. Forecasting what's next, we miss *the present moment*. Or, as John Lennon put it, "Life is what happens to you while you're busy making other plans."

As an innovation provocateur for more than 25 years, working with some of the world's most forward-thinking organizations, I've experienced quite a few *moments of truth* on the job, moments when the mundane realities of 9-5 gave way to the timeless – moments when a kind of Red Sea parted and I saw (or felt) something extraordinary. My clients hired me to do "X" (lead a workshop, give a keynote, spark a culture of innovation) and "Y" happened. But even though "Y" was not on the agenda, it was the catalyst for tremendous insight and learning.

Fascinated by the *riches under the pillow* phenomenon, I sat down one day, four years ago, and recalled 38 of these moments, shedding light on what I was learning on the job beyond providing my clients with their so-called "deliverables."

I am not the only one having these experiences. You are, too. All of us have stories to tell – stories with the power to help us see that we are not only working, but also being *worked on*.

To peel the curtain back on this phenomenon, I offer my 38 stories for your reflection – moments of truth I've experienced on the job (and elsewhere) that have revealed something profound to me. Stories of awakening. Stories of insight. Stories I hope my own children will tell one day *in addition to their own*. A brief reflection on each story's possible meaning follows the story itself plus a few questions for you to consider that will help you apply the message to your own life.

The ultimate intention of this book, however, is not to celebrate me. It's to celebrate *you*. I'm just getting the party started. That's why I've included several essays in the second part of the book that explore *why* story is such a powerful medium and *how* you can identify, shape, and communicate your own wisdom stories. I trust that this combination will not only inspire you to humanize your own work life, but also unleash the extraordinary potential of each and every experience that you have.

Revolution? Maybe. *Revelation*? For sure.

I'm From Woodstock, Yes I Am!

I'm from Woodstock. Yes, *that* Woodstock. The famous Woodstock – the most famous small town in the world. Former home to Bob Dylan. Jimi Hendrix also lived here for a summer. Levon Helm lived two miles from my place before his recent passing. John Sebastian *still* lives here, and so do a lot of other awesome musicians, artists, writers, healers, therapists, car mechanics, plumbers, electricians, and just about anyone else you'd expect to find living in a small town.

Other than winter lasting six weeks too long, I love where I live. I've been a resident for 21 years and am proud to call it my home.

Since hailing from Woodstock does not quite have the same business panache as hailing from New York, London, or Dubai, if I tell people I live in Woodstock, I run the risk of not only being stereotyped as a counter culture whack job, but being in cahoots with an entire generation of freaks for whom the word "corporation" is second only to "military industrial complex" on the list of buzz kills – a declaration fully capable of leaving my inquisitor-of-the-moment with the impression that I am either highly unqualified to be of value to his organization or a candidate to be paid in 100 pound bags of chickpeas.

Having weighed the pros and cons of my geographical pronouncement options, I decided, early in my career, to take the low road. With a big mortgage and two small children, I saw no reason to scare away possible clients.

"Two hours north of Manhattan" was my standard response. "Upstate New York" was my backup, closely followed by "the Hudson Valley," "65 miles south of Albany," and the always dependable, "foothills of the Catskill Mountains".

Whatever euphemism I used worked like a charm. People nodded their heads, asked if I wanted another glass of wine, or simply changed the subject. A thrilling conversation? Not exactly. But at least I didn't run the risk of decreasing my perceived value in the eyes of those who controlled the big budgets.

So there I was in Munich at the International Headquarters of Allianz, one of the world's leading financial services institutions with 142,000 employees and billions in sales.

My task? To lead a workshop the next day for the company's hard-driving senior leadership team to energize their newly launched effort to "gain a competitive edge by maximizing innovation."

Corporate speak? Sure. But so what? It didn't matter to me what euphemisms my clients used to express themselves. If they demonstrated even the slightest willingness to go beyond the status quo, I was there.

There, in this case, was the well-appointed, pre-dinner reception for Allianz's senior team and a handful of outside consultants like me, who had been flown in from God knows where to help the organization reach its ambitious goals.

The dress code? *Business casual.* The bar? *Open.* The client? Dutifully introducing me to anyone within his field of vision.

And so it went for an hour – the small talk, the head nods, the handshakes – me patiently waiting for the waiter with the pizza puffs and the inevitable moment when the "Where do you live?" question would head its ugly rear.

And head its ugly rear it did – the question asked somewhere between my first and second glass of chilled 1987 Riesling, me standing in a small circle of large men – Guenther, Heinrich, and Hans – three upstanding gentleman to whom I'd been introduced just minutes before.

But then an odd thing happened. I opened my mouth to say "Two hours north of Manhattan," and "*Woodstock*" came out. *Woodstock!*

Maybe it was the wine... or the jet lag... or maybe it was the cumulative effect of my 17 years of lame geographical euphemisms. Whatever it was, I knew that the next moment was going to be interesting.

For three very long German seconds, no one said a thing. The word just hovered in the air like a Super Bowl blimp. Guenther was the first to speak.

"Wow!" he exclaimed. "Did you actually *go* to the festival?"

Hans inched closer. "My older cousin went. Lucky bastard. I was too young."

Heinrich just stood there, silent as the clam dip. Then he raised his right hand with a laugh and gave me a rousing high five. "I *love* Joe Cocker!"

Somehow, I could tell that tomorrow's innovation workshop was going to be just fine.

So What?

The older I get, the more I realize there is only one thing I can do to make a difference in the world, and that is to *speak my truth with love and respect* for all the people I am speaking it to. Compared to that, everything else I could say is a distant second – poorly written dialogue in a "B" movie, tinged with fear, gamesmanship, jive, hustle, and projection.

Most of us think we have something to *lose* if we speak our truth, assuming that no one *really* wants to hear what we have to say and, if they did, we'd become hopeless outcasts, homeless former employees living in a cardboard box, with no access to cappuccino or crème brulee.

Far too many of us are stuck in survival mode on the job. Afraid of getting laid off, pissing someone off, or, if we are self-employed, losing the gig, we play it safe. Instead of playing to win, we play *not* to lose. Instead of pulling the sword from the stone, we beat around the bush. We don't just hide our light under a bushel; we hide the bushel under a mountain of excuses.

What would our work life be like or, for that matter, what would our whole life be like, if we each came out of the closet and spoke our truths – to ourselves, to each other, to our clients, managers, customers, co-workers, and anyone else who will listen? Not to prove a point. Not to vent. Not to blame. *To elevate the conversation.* Life is too short for anything else. The world needs you to be you and me to be me, not who the people "in power" think we *should* be.

Now What?

What is your version of my Woodstock story? What truth about you and your life have you been hiding under a bushel? And when will you commit to telling it like it is?

It All Began with Balls

Most companies begin on a shoestring – under-funded, under the gun, and under the radar. The company I co-founded, Idea Champions, was no exception. When my business partner and I began, we had very little – just an idea, some chutzpah, and a deep desire to succeed. While we both were likable, smart, and good schmoozers, we had almost nothing in the way of a marketing plan. We knew we had to do something beyond the tedious buying of mailing lists, but what? Racking what was left of our over-caffeinated brains, we soon realized that we needed some kind of showcase, a place to strut our entrepreneurial stuff and get the attention of prospective clients.

Back in those days, this meant one thing: renting a booth at the American Society for Training & Development (ASTD) convention. The thought of this made both of us slightly nauseous. We had attended this event once before and came away with three conclusions:

1. Every booth was boring;

2. Vendors actually expected to bring in business by giving away Hershey Kisses, and

3. We probably *should* have gone into our fathers' businesses.

Clearly, we'd have to do something unique if we were going to distinguish ourselves from the 600-plus other companies who were vying for the same customers.

Handing out slick brochures was out of the question. We didn't have any. Giving prospects our client list was also out of the question. You could count the number of our clients on one hand – the hand of Vinny "Three Finger" Scalucci. Bottom line, we would need to walk the talk, even if we were barefoot.

In a flash of mania, the two of us realized we'd need a lot of balls to pull this off. Yes, *those* kind, but also another kind – *juggling balls*. The aha? We'd teach people to juggle. Our booth would become a kind of anti-booth – a place for convention-weary people to recuperate from all the other booths.

We knew how to juggle and we knew how to teach people to juggle. The few clients we had loved it. They had fun. They got out of their heads. And they got meaningful insights into their own creative process.

Our plan was simple. We'd bring a posse of juggling-savvy friends with us and teach thousands of convention-goers how to juggle. No hard sell. No corporate speak. No used car salesman smiles, just the experience of sparking breakthroughs. Our message would be delivered in 30 seconds or less. As aspiring jugglers dropped the balls, we'd drop in a few well-timed comments to help them make the link between juggling and what it *really* takes to innovate.

For three days we taught countless people how to juggle. Some succeeded. Some did not. But everyone had a good time. Our booth was wildly popular and always attracted a crowd, but attracting a crowd does not necessarily translate into sales. Though we were pumped, we still had nothing to show for our efforts, only an entrepreneurial buzz. That is, until the afternoon of the third day.

That's when we spied the proverbial big fish walking in our direction. DIRECTOR OF TRAINING & DEVELOPMENT, AT&T, his nametag declared.

This was the moment – the moment of truth.

The impeccably dressed Mr. Big approached. He stopped, did his best to look through me, and spoke: "What is this?" he asked.

"What does it look like?" I replied.

"Juggling?"

"That's right!" I responded. "Would you like to learn?"

Ah.... the moment of choice was upon him! Dare he lay down his plastic bags full of information to try something new? Dare he stop being in charge and become a student for a change? Dare he run the risk of appearing foolish in front of total strangers?

He looked at me. I looked at him. Then he cleared his throat.

"I've been trying to learn to juggle for 25 years," he confessed, looking at his watch. "I'm in... but all I have is five minutes."

By the grace of the juggling gods, we taught him. In five minutes, this man achieved something he hadn't been able to achieve in a quarter of a century. Smiling broadly, he reached into his pocket and pulled out a business card.

"I *still* don't know what you guys do," he laughed, "but I know you're not a juggling company. Call me on Monday."

We did. He took our call and spent the next 30 minutes waxing poetic about his weekend juggling adventures. Then he started grilling us about our work. Apparently, he liked what he heard, because the next thing we knew he'd invited us to pilot our creative thinking course at AT&T.

It was a huge hit. Our now juggling-savvy client invited us back twice more the next few months to make sure the glowing feedback we'd received was not a "false positive."

It wasn't. The second and third trainings were also wildly successful. So much so that Mr. New-Juggler-After-25-Years-of Frustration pulled the corporate trigger and licensed our program. We taught nine AT&T trainers how to facilitate the course. Then, when Lucent Technologies split off from AT&T, we taught their trainers and enjoyed five years of great results and even greater passive income.

How did it all begin? By differentiating ourselves from the competition. By leveraging our strengths. By translating theory into practice. By giving people an *experience*, not just words. And by translating all of the above into a service that delivered on its promise. Balls got us started, but it was skillful execution that sealed the deal.

SO WHAT?

There are many things, in this world, that people don't agree on – like the best way to lose weight, how to end world hunger, and why some men still wear bowties. But perhaps the biggest source of disagreement is what constitutes an "intelligent risk", especially in the realm of business. After 27 years of study and hands-on experience, I think Paul Simon's lyrics best describe this phenomenon: "One man's ceiling is another man's floor." In other words, there's no formula for determining what constitutes an intelligent risk. It's all subjective.

What I do know is this: *every one of us has a gift –* something we innately do well that differentiates us from the competition and, if skillfully expressed, has the potential to be of great service. Unfortunately, most of us don't trust this gift, labeling it "irrelevant" or "unprofessional" or any number of other pejorative adjectives that diminish its value.

Clearly, at that ASTD conference, experiential learning gave my company a competitive edge – something beyond slick marketing materials and the ability to rent an expensive looking booth. Since we could not compete on a level playing field, we had to tilt the playing field. We were a horse of a different color on a planet in a different solar system. It was only when we accepted this and were willing to express our unique abilities that doors began opening for us.

NOW WHAT?

What is your competitive edge at work – something unique you bring to the table? What risks are you willing to take, this month, to express it?

The Afghani Cab Driver
and the $250 Million Dollar
Salty Snack Food

I am getting into the backseat of a Yellow cab, as I've done a thousand times before, having just tipped the too-smiling bellboy too much for holding open the door and inviting me, as he had just been trained to do last week, to "have a nice day."

Here, 1,500 miles from home, at 6:30 a.m. in front of yet another nameless business hotel, I settle into position, careful not to spill my coffee on my free copy of *USA Today*.

In 20 minutes, I will be arriving at the international headquarters of General Mills, creators of Cheerios, Wheaties, and the totally fictional fifties icon of American motherhood,

Betty Crocker. My mission? To help their product development team come up with a new $250 million dollar salty snack food.

It's too dark to read and I'm too caffeinated to nap, so I glance at the dashboard and notice a fuzzy photo of my driver, his last name next to it – an extremely long and unpronounceable last name, as if a crazed bingo master had thrown all the letters of the alphabet into a brown paper bag, shaken it, and randomly pulled each letter out in between shots of cheap tequila. I had no clue where he was from.

"Hello," I say, anxious that my driver with the long last name would end up getting us lost. "I'm on my way to General Mills. Do you... know where that is?"

"Oh yes," he replies with an accent I assume to be Middle Eastern, "I know."

Small talk out of the way, I have three choices – the same three choices I have every time I get into the backseat of a cab on the way to a meeting.

I could check my email. I could review my notes. Or I could continue the conversation with my driver, always a risky proposition, especially with cabbies from foreign lands who are often difficult to understand, tired, or, seemingly angry with Americans. This, I am not proud to say, has often led me to become much too polite, overcompensating for who knows how many years of my government's pre-emptive strikes – a response, I'm sure even the least sophisticated cab driver could see through in a heartbeat.

"Where are you from?" my driver asks.

"Woodstock," I reply. "Woodstock, New York. And you?"

"Afghanistan."

Deep as we were in the middle of that war, I am stunned, my own backseat brand of battle fatigue gathering itself for the appropriate response.

"Afghanistan?" I reply. "What brought you here?"

I could tell by his pause – his long, pregnant pause – that things were just about to change.

"Well..." my driver says, looking at me in the rearview mirror, "I was out for a walk with my 10-year old daughter when she stepped on a land mine."

I look out the window. Starbucks. McDonald's. Pier 1 Imports.

"So I ripped off my shirt and tied it around her leg to stop the bleeding. Then I went running for a doctor. But there was no doctor."

For the next 20 minutes, he tells me about his three-day journey through the mountains of Afghanistan, his bleeding daughter on his back, slipping in and out of consciousness.

Villagers took them in, gave them food, applied centuries worth of home remedies, but no one knew of a doctor.

And then... a break. A man on horseback told him of some nurses from the Mayo Clinic who had just set up an outpost only a mile up the road.

With his last bit of energy, he got there and collapsed. The nurses managed to keep his daughter alive and flew her, the next day, to the Mayo Clinic in Minneapolis. Three days later, he and his wife were flown to be by her side and they entered a yearlong rehabilitation process, so their daughter could learn to walk with her new prosthetic leg.

"That will be $27.55," my driver announces, checking the meter.

I just sit there, taking it all in. Then I thank him, pay, and make my way to the meeting room on the ninth floor.

An hour later, 15 product development specialists, large cups of coffee in hand, take their seat, waiting for the session to begin. I have a choice to make. Do I dismiss my journey from hotel to headquarters as a surreal preamble to the day? Or, do I realize that this morning's journey *is* the work at hand – a story not only for me, but also for everyone in the room that day?

So What?

This is the choice each of us needs to make every day of our lives. Do we play it safe and do the expected or do we take a risk and try something new? On that fateful day at General Mills, I could have easily dismissed my early morning cab ride as a surreal moment in time, a distraction from the business at hand. Too focused on earning my keep, I could easily have listened half-heartedly to my driver, or never have started a conversation in the first place. Afraid to ruffle feathers, I could have simply kept the story to myself. But I didn't.

The 15 General Mills people loved the story. They loved the fact that I started with something real, something human, something that *moved* them. Listening took precedence over judging. Curiosity took precedence over knowing. Gratitude took precedence over complaint. And even though there seemed

16

to be no logical segue from my cab ride to the world of General Mills, there was. The segue, in fact, was effortless. "A curious thing happened to me on my way from my hotel to this room this morning" was the only segue I needed. And what was waiting for us on the other side of that segue was a much greater sense of possibility, perseverance, and courage – three timeless qualities my cab driver had in spades – three qualities that every one of us non-Afghanis in the room that day needed more of in our lives. Could I have used the story as a way to invite General Mills to donate some of its profits to the de-mining of Afghanistan? Yes, I could have. Could I have used the story as a way to encourage General Mills to feed third world countries instead of contributing to America's obesity problem? Yes, I could have done that, too. Perhaps on a different day, I would have. But on *this* day, it was enough just to tell the story.

NOW WHAT?

Think of an unexpected encounter you've had in the past year that really moved you. What was it? And when, in the next few days, might telling this story be the perfect thing to do?

17

Do You Have Time To Catch My Bubbles?

One morning a few years ago, I found myself standing in my closet, madly searching for clean clothes in a last minute attempt to pack before yet another business trip, when I noticed my 4-year old son standing in the entrance. In one hand he held a small plastic wand, in the other, a plastic bottle of soapy water.

"Dada," he said, looking up at me, eyes wide open. "Do you have time to catch my bubbles?"

Time? It stopped. And so did I. At that moment it made no difference whether or not I caught my plane; I could barely catch my breath. The only thing that existed was my son and that soulful look of longing in his eyes.

For the next ten minutes, all we did was play – him blowing bubbles and laughing, me catching bubbles and laughing, too.

His need was completely satisfied. His need for connection. His need for love. His need for knowing, beyond a shadow of a doubt, that his daddy was there for him and everything was perfect just the way it was.

Jesse is 21 now. His bubbles are digital. But his need – and mine – are still the same.

So What?

This just in: *The business of life is not a life of business.* There is something going on beyond spreadsheets, profit margins, and fourth-quarter projections that is worthy of our attention. Like love, for example. Like kindness. Like caring, fun, forgiveness, and being totally present with the people in your life – especially those who live under the roof you are working so hard to make sure remains over their head.

Somehow, along the way, we have forgotten that *earning a living* is not the same thing as *living* – that the people counting on us for survival are more interested in our interest in them than the compounded interest we are trying to earn for them.

This is tricky business, especially in a down economy when it takes a whole lot more effort than ever to make the same amount of money you used to make.

On that memorable day in my closet, if you asked me what I was doing the moment before Jesse asked me to catch his bubbles, I would have given you a stock answer – something like, "getting ready for a road trip" or "packing." If you'd pressed me, I might have said something like "building a house of bricks" for my family.

My son didn't want to play with bricks that day. He wanted to play with bubbles. Bubbles were not a part of his long-term strategy. They were a crystal clear invitation for me to stop doing what I was doing and be with him *in the moment* – the moment my son was living in and I was planning for.

Now What?

Who has been blowing bubbles your way recently? Have you acknowledged them? Rethought your priorities? Given them your attention? If not, pause for a moment and consider a few ways you can catch their bubbles this week.

THE POETRY OF LIFE

There is a moment in everyone's life when all the cards are on the table, all the chips, too – the moment of truth when the entire universe, it seems, is conspiring to call one's attention to the choice we have every day to let go of the past and move towards what is calling us, even if we have no idea where it will lead.

One such moment happened for me in 1969, during my first and only semester as a graduate student at Brown University's prestigious MFA Creative Writing Program.

Like other long-haired, Vietnam-phobic seekers of truth whose Depression-imprinted parents would have much preferred him to have chosen law, medicine, or the Talmud over poetry, I found myself, at the ripe old age of 22, sleeping 12 hours a day, posting my poems on trees at midnight, and feverishly reading Rilke, Wallace Stevens, and William Carlos Williams. All this in case any number of my far more well-read poetry professors engaged me in esoteric literary conversations at any number of ultra-hip faculty parties I kept getting invited to – the kind of heady gatherings where Kurt Vonnegut and other travelling bards kept showing up, laugh lines around their eyes unable to mask a lifetime's worth of sadness and despair.

At one of these high-octave, Ivy League literary soirees one autumn night, emboldened by whatever intoxicants I could get my hands on, I was overtaken by a single question rising from my loins – the kind of question that, if unspoken, might have devolved the rest of my life into a pitiful charade – everything I ended up writing being, at best, nothing more than clever overcompensation for my chicken shit silence.

Approaching my first professor, large glass of wine in hand, I let it fly, "If you could be anywhere in the world, at this precise moment, where would you be?"

"Hmm…" my professor replied, dramatically pausing just in case a beautiful co-ed was standing nearby. "Excellent question! Let me see, if I could be anywhere in the world at this moment in time where would it be? Well, that would be… Baja, California. Definitely Baja, California. Feels like home to me."

Nodding appreciatively and doing my bearded, graduate-student best not to bump into anyone as I crossed the now tilting room, I sought out my second professor, an unhappily married, hammock-bellied man who I knew was hitting on the same unhappily married shopkeeper in town that I was.

"Guatemala!" he blurted. "Oh yes, Guatemala, especially that sweet, little village 30 miles outside of the capital city. Can't remember the name. Love that place!"

Fueled as I was by what was now emerging as a definable pattern of response, I found my way to the bar where Professor #3 was holding court, a large hummus stain on his too-small polyester shirt.

"Where would I be if I could be anywhere in the world?" he repeated. "Easy! The Pacific Northwest. The rain! The fog! What a fabulous place to write. You really need to visit sometime, Mitch."

As I walked away, 22-year-old-knowingly, to the last of the lot, Professor #4, it began to dawn on me that none of my so-called mentors wanted to be where they were! All of them wanted to be somewhere else – a better place, a different place, a more exotic place, but not where we were standing. And here I was, aspiring to be just like them – published, tenured, and respected – when 20 years later some wise-ass graduate student would ask where I wanted to be and my answer would be *somewhere else.*

Why not leave now while I still could?

I slept well that night and the next night, too, fully rested for my Monday morning class, the one Professor #1 began by calling my name, noting with tenured gravitas that he wanted to see me immediately after class, a request that could mean only one thing – *the jig was up,* and that I, Mr. Attempt-to-Outstare-My-Professors-So-They-Would-Think-I-Knew-More-Than-I-Did, was about to be summarily kicked out of school, underwhelmed as my teachers were by the spotty quality of my work and the

25

insidious ways in which Lawrence Ferlinghetti kept leaking into my writing, not to mention the fact that I still had no clue what the big deal was about Wallace Stevens.

"Mr. Ditkoff," Professor #1 intoned as the class emptied out, "the faculty and I... after reviewing your work carefully... have unanimously decided to give you a full teaching scholarship."

"That's interesting," I replied. "I quit."

"Quit?" he replied. "You can't quit. Don't you realize what you're being given here – a full teaching scholarship – an absolutely free education at one of the best graduate schools in the world?"

"Like I said, sir, I quit. My education needs to happen somewhere else."

Two days later I was gone. Two weeks after that I was living where I really wanted to live, Cambridge, Massachusetts, doing what I really wanted to do: being a night desk clerk at a second rate hotel, working the midnight shift, with plenty of time to *live* the poetry of life, not forcing myself to write about it.

So What?

While I'm open to the possibility that "the world is my oyster," sometimes a grilled cheese sandwich is more in order or, better yet, fasting. Just because the world is dangling a shiny object in front of us doesn't necessarily mean we should grab it. No one knows for sure whether that shiny object is "right," "wrong," "grace," or "temptation." In the end, it all comes down to *gut feel* and our own sense of what's calling us. You can throw the *I-Ching* all you want, ask your closest friends for their sage counsel, and convene focus groups until you're blue in the face, but ultimately it all comes down to you and your ability to tune into what moves you. When you trust *that*, doors open. Minds, too.

Now What?

What is your "poetry of life" choice at the moment? At what crossroads are you standing? What decision is up for you right now? And what can you do to increase your odds of making the choice that will have the best possible outcome for you?

How a Big Idea Opens Doors

It was not a mystery to me, how I ended up on the 50-yard line of Mile High Stadium two hours before the high-flying Denver Broncos were about to play the Oakland Raiders in the 1978 AFC Championship game, one that would determine who would go to the Super Bowl. It was a testament to the power of a big idea.

Two months prior, while meditating in my low-rent Denver apartment, a fascinating thought welled up from deep within me or wherever fascinating thoughts well up from – the first bubble, it seemed, of a perfectly chilled bottle of champagne I had no memory of opening.

BIG. The idea was big. Very big. And all I had to do was make two phone calls to make it happen.

The first? To *Denver Magazine*, to inform them I had an exclusive interview scheduled (I didn't) with The Pony Express, the Broncos' super hot cheerleading squad. The second? To the Denver Broncos, to let them know that I was a writer with *Denver Magazine* (I wasn't) and ready to do a cover story on the Pony Express.

In my mind, this was a done deal. Like the sun coming up tomorrow. Or the dishes in my sink remaining there for at least another week.

So I picked up the phone and called the editor of *Denver Magazine*. He loved the idea, committed on the spot, and gave me two timely bits of information: what my compensation would be and when the article was due. Then I called the Broncos' PR Director. He loved the idea, too, and also gave me two bits of information: the phone number of the head cheerleader and the location of their next rehearsal.

I was in! I was on! Or whatever the right preposition was to express the championship delight I was feeling.

My job? To watch 23 professional cheerleaders go through their shimmy, shake, and grind routines once a week, then interview them, looking for clues beyond their extraordinary cleavage, to determine if they had anything enlightening to say to the readers of *Denver Magazine*.

This went on for a month until I knew all their names, all their moves, and all their career aspirations – high-flying dreams of the future that seemed to escalate with each passing day.

"Would you like to ride on the bus with us to the Raider game?" the head cheerleader asked me after the third rehearsal. "It should give you some new angles for the story."

Angles? Curves? It was all the same to me, watching, as I was, with great fascination, my now four-week old idea continuing to take shape on a national stage.

Sitting in the back of the bus on game day, marveling at the number of cordless hair dryers able to operate simultaneously at 60 miles per hour, I couldn't help but wonder *how* I was going to get past the security guards when we finally got to the stadium, me a man with no credentials, no press pass, no union card, not even a letter of introduction.

Then the head cheerleader stood, told us we'd reached our destination, and provided the last few words of encouragement as we filed out, moving like a great sea of bangles, beads, and breasts to the final security checkpoint.

Two by two the cheerleaders were waved through. Two by two, I was getting closer to the realization of my BIG IDEA, heart pounding, palms sweating, feeling increasingly unofficial.

"Hey Stacey," I call to the cheerleader walking next to me, "give me your pom-poms."

She does. The line grows shorter and so does my breath, the crustiest of security guards trying his best to look through me.

"HEY!" he barks to the last few cheerleaders, "Who's *that* guy?"

"Oh, him!" they chant in unison. *"He's with us!"*

I smile, shake my pom-poms, and keep walking. I'm in!

The girls go their way and I go mine, which is where any self-respecting 29-year-old sports enthusiast and his big idea would go: *mid-field* – the 50-yard line – the smack dab center of the football universe.

Up some staircases, down some ramps, through some hallways, out a chain-linked gate, and I am on the field.

No linebackers are pursuing me. No cornerbacks. No safeties. The field is wide open and so am I, moving as fast as I can, tape recorder tucked under my arm, to the 50-yard line.

Off in the distance, I see a large man in a dark uniform making his way towards me. His uniform is not orange like the Broncos. It is not silver and black like the Raiders. It is blue. Dark blue. Policeman blue.

If there was ever going to be an ESPN highlight reel of my life, this moment would be in it, the large officer of the law fast approaching, the only visible obstacle between me and my heart's destination.

Seeing he was just about to speak, I extend my microphone in his direction and position it just a few inches from his face.

"Officer," I announce in the most resonant prime-time news voice I can muster, "Can we get your prediction? Who's going to win today?"

The policeman pauses, making sure he is talking directly into the microphone. "Are you kidding me?" he blurts. "The Broncos! 27-10!"

Cupping my ear, I look up to the mythical press box in the mythical distance and announce, "You heard it folks, *live from Officer Willoughby* at Mile High Stadium. Broncos, 27. Raiders, 10. Now back to you, Ed."

The officer continues on his way. I jog the final few yards to the 50-yard line, TV technicians scurrying all around me. The air is brisk. The sky is blue. The big game is about to begin.

So What?

Some people say the entire universe is just an idea in the mind of God. While that is certainly possible, I cannot prove it, nor can you, so I won't pursue that line of thinking. What I will say is this: ideas are powerful. Whether you believe in "the mind of God" or not, it's reasonable to believe that the things we create begin as ideas in our mind. The idea is the beginning of all things.

Now What?

Jot down three intriguing ideas you've had in the past few months that you would like to see manifest. For the moment, suspend your judgment of how practical these ideas are or how difficult it will be to pull them off. Just write them down. Don't decide anything yet. Just brew on them for a while. Entertain them. Give them some air to breathe.

THE MAN WITH THE METAL TEETH

I knew I was in trouble the moment he smiled. All I could see were four metal teeth – the *front* ones – the ones people use to bite things. Like an apple. Or a cracker. Or the head of a consultant teaching a course on creative thinking.

His nametag said "John Andrews," but when it was time to introduce himself to the group, it was "Master Staff Sergeant John Andrews, Fourth Battalion."

Apparently, the man with the metal teeth was still fighting the Vietnam War – and, by the look in his eye, it was clear he couldn't tell what side I was on. Unlike the other 20 people in the room dressed in "business casual," John wore a suit and a tie, a tie tied so tight I thought the veins in his neck would burst.

I took a breath and invited John to remove his tie and jacket, explaining that *relaxation* was one of the pre-conditions for creativity. John declined.

This man was not the first tough cookie I'd encountered in corporate America. Like ridiculous CEO bonuses, it comes with the territory. Over the years, I've learned to embrace people like John. He was not the enemy. Without going out of my way to win him over, he was simply someone I would need to be aware of as the day unfolded. In the end, everything would be fine – or so I told myself.

John was probably the same way with me as he was with his wife, children, and administrative assistant. He had mastered the fine art of making people uncomfortable. For him, it was a survival skill, a pre-emptive strike that set the tone for all his interactions – his way of letting people know who was really in charge.

At no time during the next two days did Master Sergeant John Andrews, Fourth Battalion give the slightest indication that he was receiving any value from the session I was leading. Not a nod. Not a smile. Not a clue. Indeed, if I had been his Vietcong interrogator, John would have chosen not to divulge the number of men in his battalion.

He seemed very skilled at keeping secrets.

When the training ended, the participants were out the door in a flash. No one lingered. No one except Master Sergeant John Andrews, Fourth Battalion, still wearing his tie.

"Do you… need… any help cleaning up?" he asked.

"Yes, I do, John. That would be great. Thanks."

Silently, both of us got busy picking stuff up off the floor.

Two minutes into it, John, now on his hands and knees, looked up at me.

"I… um… wonder if I can have a few minutes of your time?" he asked. "I need some help."

Seeing this proud man on his hands and knees, looking at me with a mix of fear and sadness, was not an image I had conjured when he first bared his four metal teeth two days before. Still kneeling, he went on to tell me that his direct reports had just completed their 360-degree evaluations of him and the results were "not good." Apparently, his job was on the line.

I don't remember what I said to John. All I know is that whatever I said rang true for him. It had nothing to do with creativity or innovation. *It had a lot to do with life.* John's life. My life and all our lives. The stuff that is *really* important. Not titles. Not spreadsheets. Not data, profits, headcount, technology, or promotions. None of that. It had to do with the *spirit* in which we do things. Not the *what* of life, but the *how.* The difference between a life of business and the business of life.

Time seemed to stop for the two of us in that room. For the next 30 seconds neither of us said a word. We just stood there, stunned. Then John turned to me and asked if it would be OK if he took a second set of juggling balls home to his 14-year old son.

So What?

I am not a particularly religious person. Although I do consider myself, a "man of the spirit," I have never been a big fan of rites, rituals, and all the other cosmological flora and fauna that comes with the territory of organized religion. That being said, there is something about religion that I love: the stories – the timeless parables embedded with the DNA of universal truth. One of my favorite comes from Christianity – the story of how only a few people in Jesus's time recognized that he had anything special going on for him – a not surprising phenomenon when you consider that he looked like a hippie, worked as a carpenter, created havoc in the temples, and fit absolutely none of the pundit's predictions of what Mr. Big would do or say.

And so it was with Staff Sergeant John T. Andrews of the Fourth Battalion.

The paradox? I was teaching a class on how to get out of the box, but my judgments of John only created a bigger box around him than the one he was already in. Then, he didn't just need to get out of his own box; he needed to get out of the box I had created around his box.

Thankfully, I chose early in the session to relate to the *best* part of John – even if *he* wasn't willing or able to see the best in anyone else, especially me. My intention? To be more committed to *inclusion* than *conclusion*.

It wasn't easy being with him. It wasn't fun. But it *was* an effort well worth it – the effort to have more faith in John than he had in himself. And while John may have thanked me for helping him get out of the box, *he helped me get out of my own* – my box of thinking I knew what was possible for two days in a room with 20 AT&T employees – none of whom I remember today except Sergeant John T. Andrews, Fourth Battalion.

So What?

In your place of business, this same phenomenon is playing out daily in a thousand different ways. Everyone you work with has a little bit of John in them. Everyone, in their own way, is stuck, contorted, contracted, anxious, uptight, wounded, aggressive, habitual, confronting, controlling, remote, self-absorbed, projecting, and unkind. But beyond what people look like and act like, is also an open, caring, creative, expressive, hopeful, adaptive, humble, sincere, loving, soulful, high-potential human being.

If you, as a manager, teammate, colleague, or coach are willing to suspend your knee- jerk judgments of the Johns of the world, it's only a matter of time before your team or organization becomes a place where everyone thrives, everyone grows, and everyone – *yes, everyone* – can't wait to get out of bed in the morning to come to work.

Now What?

Who, in the workplace, might you be judging too harshly? Who might you be putting in a box because of the way they act? Who have you given up on that, with just a little more care and attention, might get the breakthrough needed to make the valuable contribution you know they are capable of?

THE POOL PLAYER

All of us tell stories, even if we don't think of ourselves as storytellers. And the plots of our stories are about anything and everything: our day, how we met our spouse, found God, lost our virginity, or why the fender bender was the other guy's fault. Most of the stories we tell tend to be our own, but not all of them. Some stories we tell are other people's.

If you've ever told a fairy tale, recounted a parable from your favorite scripture, or repeated something cool that happened to your best friend, you are telling someone else's story. This is not plagiarism. Nor is it an indication your stories aren't as good as theirs. All it means is that something in you has resonated with a story you've heard from someone else and are inspired to pass it on. That's precisely what rabbis, priests, and teachers from all of the great spiritual traditions have done since the beginning of time – tell other people's stories, the most effective way to give shape to the timeless truths they want to communicate to a world deeply in need of healing and wisdom.

What follows is one of these stories. It is not my story, but my father's, a man who was a fantastic storyteller, so taken by his own narratives that it was not uncommon for him to tell me the same story 20 times or more. At first, his repetitive storytelling used to bug me, big time, as in "Hey Dad, I already heard that one," but as I got older, I began to realize that a good story, like a good piece of music or a beautiful piece of art, could be experienced again and again and again – that it wasn't just about "the point" being made, but the feeling that came from listening.

When my father was a student at the Brooklyn College of Pharmacy, he became friends with a guy named "Solly," a fellow student who was an avid pool player. Every day, after class, Solly would make his way to the pool room at the end of a long hallway only to find that all the tables had been taken by classmates who had gotten there first. No matter how quickly Solly walked from his class to the pool room, by the time he got there the tables were occupied, leaving him with only one option – to watch – not at all what he wanted to do.

Necessity being the mother of invention (and the patron saint of pool sharks), Solly soon realized he'd have to do something different, next semester, in order get a table. So he decided to sign up for whatever class was held immediately adjacent to the pool room so he could play pool after class. That was his goal. That was his mission.

When Solly found out that the class adjacent to the pool room was "The History of the Bible," he began laughing hysterically, as that was the last class in the world he would ever have signed up for, but sign up he did.

Solly's plan worked like a charm. Every day, after class, for the next semester, he was the first one in the pool room and had his pick of tables. He played pool every day and his game improved immensely. What he didn't count on, however, was how fascinating the History of the Bible class was going to be. So fascinating, in fact, that Solly signed up for the advanced class the next semester (which, by the way, was nowhere near the pool room). One more Bible History class after that and Solly changed his major, eventually going on to graduate school in Religious Studies and, some years after that, becoming one of the most renowned Bible scholars in the world.

So What?

As the story goes, a similar thing happened to Steve Jobs. Disgruntled with the education he was getting at Reed College, Steve dropped out of school but stayed on campus to audit classes. One of the classes he audited was calligraphy, a subject that not only fascinated him but also laid the foundation, years later, for the Macintosh to become the first personal computer to give users a choice of cool fonts. Bottom line, we never really know what influences are at play in our lives, what seemingly illogical, random, serendipitous choices we make that will have impact. There are mysterious forces at work, for each of us – forces that are not immediately visible to us. It doesn't matter if you call it "karma," "synchronicity," "serendipity," "happenstance," or "God's play." The fact of the matter is: the path is not always straight and narrow. There is magic afoot, but we need to let go and allow this magic to unfold.

Now What?

Think of one, off-the-grid moment in your life that had great impact for you – a chance meeting, a happy accident, or an unexplainable synchronicity. How did that moment affect your life? What did you learn from it? And whom, in the next week, will you share this story with?

THE UPTOWN BEGGAR

I have never been fired from a job. Except once – a week after the man I wrote 350 speeches for in two years, Donald J. Manes, the Borough President of Queens, committed suicide in his kitchen because he knew he was just about to get busted for stealing more than one million dollars from the City of New York in what is now affectionately known as the Parking Violations Bureau scandal.

I wasn't fired because I had done anything wrong. I hadn't. I was fired because the successor to the Not-So-Honorable Donald J. Manes wanted to clean house in a B-movie politically correct way to appease the irate public's need for reform. A new leaf. She was turning over a new leaf, and a whole bunch of other metaphors being supplied to her by a newly hired PR advisor.

The bottom line? At 37, I was out of a job, unemployed, with an exorbitant Upper West Side rent due in less than a month.

Having saved almost nothing from my speech-writing gig and with absolutely no desire to write for yet another person with delusions of grandeur, I decided to go the artistic route and earn my living the honest way – playing my clarinet in the subway.

The first day I made $8.00. There was no second day.

So I did what any, self-respecting, former English Lit major with a little known ability to recite *Canterbury Tales* in Middle English would do. I wrote. Not a screenplay. Not a suicide note. But a query letter to *New York Magazine* pitching an investigative journalism article on the beggars of Manhattan – the real story, I declared, behind the people who panhandled for a living.

And so, for the next 30 days, that's exactly what I did – walked the streets of the Big Apple, doing my underground reporter best to befriend the people most of us think aren't really beggars at all but con artists trying to fool us for a living, bad actors impersonating beggars.

Thirty days I spent with them. Thirty days walking, talking, buying them lunch and trying to discover the organizing principle around which my story would authentically take shape. And I did. Find it, that is, the moment I met Fred.

His spot? 79th and Columbus, just one block from my apartment. His shtick? Pepe, his dog. Or more accurately, his *sign* for Pepe, his dog – a portable cardboard sign painstakingly printed with a pen he found three weeks ago that let the world know he wasn't begging for himself, but for his faithful companion, a ten-year old mutt he found on the street and loved too much not to feed.

Standing there before this man, tape recorder tucked under my right arm, I couldn't help but smile. This was either the cleverest of panhandler scams or Fred was an uptown saint. I looked at him and he looked at me. Then, with a crook of his head and a word I didn't understand, he signaled me to sit with him and Pepe on a blanket that had seen, shall we say, better days.

He told me his name, but not much else. We sat there, in silence, side by side, Pepe before us, as hundreds of people walked by, most casting glances, not coins. Thirty minutes passed, then Fred, with a pained look in his eye, looked at me and asked if I would "mind his dog" while he went looking for a hotel or restaurant to relieve himself.

And so, for the next hour, I sat there on the blanket with Pepe, the sign, and a tin cup. This being 79th and Columbus, many purposeful, well-dressed people walked by. All of them, of course, assumed *I* was the beggar.

"NO!" I wanted to scream. "You've got it all wrong! I'm not a beggar. I'm a writer doing a story on beggars." But I couldn't find the words. Somehow, the cat *and* the dog both had my tongue. I was speechless. And then, I got it. I finally got it. *I was a beggar.* Yes, me. I was a beggar. I was absolutely no different than Fred. I wrote stories. He wrote signs. He was trying to get money. I was trying to get money. And both of us were asking for help.

When Fred finally returned 30 minutes later he had a big wet spot on his pants.

"What happened?" I asked.

47

Fred shook his head. "No one would let me in," he explained. "I went to ten restaurants and five hotels and no one would let me in."

So What?

I still don't know if Fred was an uptown saint, a beggar with a shtick, or my cousin Lazlo from a former lifetime. What I do know is no one would let this man into their place of business to pee. What I do know is that, of the hundreds of people who walked by me while Fred searched for a place to relieve himself, less than 5% expressed any compassion. To them, Fred (and later, me) was an eyesore, an inconvenient moment on their way to wherever they were going. What I do know is that something broke open for me when I sat alone, on the blanket with Pepe. "There but for the grace of God, go I" the expression goes. But Fred could not go. No one would let him go. It wouldn't have taken much for someone to make Fred's day – a simple act of kindness… a relaxing of the rules… extending a hand in need. We are all Fred. We are all looking for relief.

Now What?

The next time you pass a beggar on the street, even if you decide not to give money, give attention. Nod. Smile. Speak an encouraging word. Don't just pass the beggar by. And, by the way, not all "beggars" dress the part. Some of them walk the hallways where you work.

THE POWER OF TEARS

Social media did not exist when I was 26. But *social work* did. As the Golden Boy of an upper middle class Jewish family from New York, social work was not on my radar. The pay wasn't good enough. The status wasn't high enough. And the hours weren't short enough. So when my neighbor, a University of Virginia Medical Center pediatrician, invited me to become the social worker for a new, federally-funded "early childhood intervention program" I was only half listening. Yes, I was *social* and yes, I knew how to work, but counseling parents of multi-handicapped infants did not seem like a talent I possessed.

My neighbor, the pediatrician, saw it differently.

"We have a mentor already picked out for you," she explained. "And besides, we don't want *professional* social workers. We want people who can learn on the job, so we can roll this program out across the country."

The case she made was compelling – for me to be part of a team of health care professionals who would provide services to families with handicapped children. The goal was to do everything possible to keep the families together – a challenge that, historically, had been difficult to do, given all of the dysfunctional behaviors that manifest when a handicapped child enters the family system.

My job? To be the first person, from our team, on the scene whenever a physically handicapped child was born at the University of Virginia Medical Center or identified, a few months later, as showing the signs of developmental delay. The protocol was a simple one. I would get a phone call from the hospital and drop everything I was doing to meet with the doctors and parents. The doctors were glad to see me because they knew I would deal with any untidy emotional issues. The parents were *not* glad to see me because my appearance confirmed that something was wrong with their child.

For two years, that's what I did. I learned a lot and felt a lot. But the one thing that stands out in my mind, some 41 years later, has nothing to do with facilitating parent groups, making home visits, or navigating the bureaucracy of a flawed medical system. It has to do with a young, single mother and the power of tears.

Lorraine Thompson was 17 when I first met her in a fluorescently lit waiting room. Her son, Michael, was three months old. Neither of them was in good shape. Lorraine was overwhelmed, highly stressed, and barely said a word. Michael twitched, kicked, and drooled, having been diagnosed with cerebral palsy just days before.

Witnessing this young woman's pain, my instinct was to comfort her, to be a safe haven from all her suffering. And so, for the first few months of our counseling sessions I brought her tea and listened, reminding her of the many resources available to her. After each session, I wrote up my notes and carefully tracked whatever progress she had made since her last visit.

It appeared progress was being made. Lorraine's mood seemed to improve. My social work mentor saw it differently, however. To her, the progress being made wasn't progress at all, but my own unconscious strategy to protect Lorraine *and myself* from what really needed to happen. My good intentions were getting in the way. What needed to happen, my mentor explained, was for me to stop being so damn benevolent and let Lorraine Thompson, the 17-year old, semi-catatonic, single mother of a severely handicapped son, *fall apart.* She had to, as my mentor explained, "fall to the place where she could fall no further from."

At first, I balked at this suggestion. Hey, I was the only person in the world from whom this young woman received any solace and now I was being asked to withdraw it? It made no sense. But, after listening to my mentor wax on about "the healing process," my task became clear. The next time I met with Lorraine, I would let her fall apart.

Three weeks passed. Lorraine and her son, as they had been accustomed to doing for months, met me in the parents' lounge. We began as we usually did, me asking Lorraine about her week. After a few minutes of chit chat, she started talking about the tough stuff – the lack of support from her mother and her son's constant gagging on food. But instead of responding with a hand on the shoulder or light-hearted diversion, I said nothing. I just sat there, silent, looking at her, no good news issuing forth from me.

Lorraine held my gaze for about 10 seconds and then started crying. The crying turned to sobbing and the sobbing turned into something I have no name for. I continued sitting there in silence, remembering the sage counsel of my mentor, "Let her fall to the place where she could fall no further from."

It took a while, but it happened. Lorraine cried all her tears. When she was done, I reached out and held her hand. At first she wouldn't look at me. Then she did, a great deal of relief in her eyes.

So What?

I wonder how much time in my life I've spent propping other people up – when all they really needed was for me to hold the space for them to let go. In the name of benevolence, compassion, and humanity, I've performed any number of seemingly heartfelt moves designed to relieve the suffering of others. And while all of it has been well-intentioned, there have been many times when the highest expression of wisdom would have been to do nothing other than "hold the space" – a space where no props and pep talks were needed – a space where healing could begin.

Now What?

Is there a Lorraine Thompson in your life – someone going through a hard time who you've been propping up with your good intentions? Who is this person? Are you willing, the next time you meet with him or her, to stop trying to save them from their pain and simply let them feel what there is to feel?

THE MARTIAL ARTS OF THE MIND

Ten years ago I was invited to teach a course on "Innovation and Business Growth" at GE's Management Development Center for 75 high potential, business superstars of the future. The GE executive who hired me was a very savvy guy with the unenviable task of orienting new adjunct faculty members to GE's high standards and often harsher reality.

My client's intelligence was exceeded only by his candor as he proceeded to tell me, in no uncertain terms, that GE gave new instructors *two shots* at making the grade –explaining, with a wry smile, that most outside consultants were intimidated the first time they taught at GE and weren't necessarily at the top of their game.

I'm not sure how you say it in Esperanto, but in English what he said translates as "the heat is on."

And so I went about my business of getting ready, keeping in mind that I was going to be leading a six-hour session for GE's best and brightest – high flying *Type A* personalities with a high regard for themselves and a very low threshold for anything they judged to be unworthy of their time.

I had five weeks to get my act together, five weeks to front-load my agenda with everything I needed to wow my audience: case studies, statistics, quotes, and best practices.

I was ready. *Really* ready. Like a rookie center fielder on designer steroids, I was ready. Or so I thought.

The more I spoke, the less they listened. The less they listened, the more I spoke, trotting out compelling facts and truckloads of information to make my case as they checked their email under their tables.

Psychologists would characterize my approach as "compensatory behavior." I talked faster. I talked louder. I worked harder – attempting in various pitiful ways to pull imaginary rabbits out of imaginary hats.

GE's best and brightest, for the entire 45 minutes of my opening act, were not impressed. My attempt to out-GE the GE people was a no-win proposition. I didn't need new facts, new statistics, or new quotes. I needed *a new approach* – a way to capture the attention. And I needed to do it five minutes, not 45.

The next few days were very uncomfortable for me, replaying in my head my lame choice of an opening gambit and wondering what I could do, next time, to get better results in much less time.

And then, it hit me. *The martial arts* – something I had been studying on and off for years.

Fast forward a few weeks.

My second session at GE began exactly like the first with the Program Director reading my bio to the group in a heroic attempt to impress everyone. Taking my cue, I walked to center stage and uttered nine words.

"Raise your hand if you're a bold risk-taker."

Not a single hand went up. Not one. I stood my ground and surveyed the room.

"Really?" I asked. "You are GE's best and brightest and not *one* of you is a bold risk-taker? I find that hard to believe."

Ten rows back, a hand went up. Slowly. Halfway. Like a kid unprepared in a high school geometry class.

"Great!" I bellowed. "Now stand up and join me in the front of the room!"

I welcomed my assistant to the stage and asked him if he had any insurance – explaining that I had called him forth to attack me from behind and was going to demonstrate a martial arts move shown to me by my first aikido instructor, a 110-pound woman who I once saw throw a 220-pound man through a wall.

Pin drop silence.

I asked our bold risk-taker to stand behind me and grab both of my wrists, instructing him to hold on tight as I tried to get away – an effort that yielded no results.

I casually mentioned that the scenario we were demonstrating exemplified a typical work day for most of us – lots of tension, resistance, and struggle.

With the audience focused on the moment, I noted a few simple principles of aikido and how anyone, with the right application of energy and practice, could change the game.

As I demonstrated the move, I neutralized my attacker and was no longer victim, but now in total control. Within two minutes, the energy had totally shifted. Not only for my attacker and me, but also for everyone in the room.

That's when I mentioned that *force* was not the same thing as *power*, that martial artists know how to get maximum results with minimum effort, and that innovation was all about the "martial arts of the mind" – a way to get extraordinary results in an elegant way.

I was invited back 26 times to deliver the course.

So What?

Every day, no matter what work we do, we are all faced with the same challenge – how to effectively communicate our message – a challenge especially difficult these days when the information available to us is doubling every ten years. Yearly, more than one million books are published. Daily, we are bombarded with more than 6,000 advertising messages and 150 emails. As a result, most of us find ourselves in a defensive posture, protecting ourselves from the onslaught of input.

What I've discovered in the past 25 years is that if I really want to get my message across, I've got to deliver it in a way that gets past the guardians at the gate – the default condition of doubt, disengagement, and derision that comes with the territory of life in the 21st century business world.

My rite of passage at GE offers a microcosm of this phenomenon. My attempt to win over my audience by impressing them with data, case studies, and best practices was a losing game. Not only was I barking up the wrong tree, I was in the wrong forest. The key to breaking through my audiences' collective skepticism wasn't a matter of information, but a matter of transformation. They didn't need to analyze; they needed to engage. I had to do something that invoked the curious, playful, and associative right brain, not the logical, linear, analytical left brain.

That's why I chose the martial arts – my attempt to move them from the Dow to the Tao, a state of mind where being involved is at least as important as being informed. In most organizations, information is no longer sufficient to spark change. Data is no longer king. Thinking takes us only part of the way home. It's feeling that completes the journey, feeling and the courage to communicate our message in a fresh, new way.

NOW WHAT?

What message have you been trying to deliver that might be better communicated in a totally different way – a way that more successfully engages people and leads to the kind of extraordinary results you're looking for?

Arm Wrestling the CIA

One good thing about being the night desk clerk at a seedy hotel is that you get to be invisible to most people. If you're looking for a place to disappear and still make a living, this is the place. To begin with, it's the *night* shift, so almost everyone else is sleeping. Secondly, the few people who are awake don't notice you. You are part of the background. Like a potted plant. Or the maximum occupancy sign.

Invisible to *most* people, however, doesn't mean invisible to *all* people and, on this particular night, the exception was the rule.

Staring at me from across the lobby was a large man – at least 6'5" – with broad shoulders, and an ill-fitting suit.

"HEY!" he shouted, walking towards me. "I don't like hippies," an obvious reference to the length of my hair.

I paid no attention, but he kept coming, moving at a gait that suggested he probably should have left the bar at least an hour ago.

"Do you know who I am?" he bellowed, now only the front desk separating us.-

"No sir, I don't," I replied.

"CIA! I'm a CIA agent."

"Oh," I said, "that's nice."

But no matter how much I ignored him, he wouldn't go away.

"I challenge you to an arm wrestle," the man declared.

"You *what?*" I replied.

"You heard me, my little hippie friend. I challenge you to an arm wrestle."

Realizing I had nothing to lose, I accepted. "OK, you're on."

Two things my soon-to-be opponent didn't know about me: first, I was a very good arm wrestler. And second, I was a student of the martial arts and had recently learned a technique known as "The Unbendable Arm," in which you imagined an endless stream of unbendable energy flowing through your arm and fingers for 10,000 miles. Done correctly, no one could bend your arm. No one.

When he put his massive arm on the desk, it was obvious I was at an extraordinary disadvantage. So, I looked straight into his beady little CIA eyes and told him the only way this contest would happen was if I put a could put few books under my elbow.

Impatient to begin, he agreed. With my free, right hand, I reached over to my night's reading and chose three: *The Complete Poems of Rilke*, the *I Ching*, and *Trout Fishing in America*.

Now, the moment of truth!

"OK, Mr. CIA," I said. "Here we go. On the count of three. 1....2....3!"

As expected, he made his power move, putting everything he had into one gigantic burst of force. But I was ready. He could not budge me.

Shocked, he tried again and still the same result. None. His third attempt also came up empty, the bulging veins in his neck the only visible proof of his effort. I could see the look of doubt in his eye.

That's when it hit me. *Now* was the perfect time for me to strike. So, I made *my* power move. Shocked I was going after him, he shifted into his own fifth gear to parry my attack. A second effort, I reasoned, made no sense. It would only weaken me. So, I did nothing. The two of us just stood there, frozen into some kind of eternal handshake mudra on the cold, faux marble-topped desk of that seedy hotel.

"Shall we call it a draw?" I asked.

He nodded, stood to his full height, and, in slow motion, backed away to the center of the lobby, holding my gaze the entire time. Then, with a sly smile, he brought his two hands together in front of his heart and bowed from the waist. Following suit, I brought *my* two hands together and bowed once to him as well.

Then he turned, walked across the lobby, pushed the elevator button, and was gone.

So What?

The image of this man, bowing to me in the middle of the lobby has been permanently burned into my mind. It is now 46 years later and I remember that moment as if it was yesterday. Unexpected as it was, it was a major teaching in my life –that standing your ground in the face of seemingly insurmountable odds is not as difficult as it may seem and that even the most negative force in the world can be transformed with the right application of attitude and energy.

Now What?

In the face of what negative force – at work, at home, or anywhere else – do you need to take a stand and come to a place of mutual respect? What does "taking a stand" actually look like to you?

Follow Your Feeling, Not the Money Trail

For the life of me, I cannot remember the name of the financial services company that left me an urgent voice mail message asking that I call them back immediately about my availability to lead their annual leadership retreat.

All I can recall is how generic sounding their name was – something like *National Investment Services...* or *Consolidated Financial Brokers....* or *The American Banking Alliance* – kind of like the corporate equivalent of John Doe.

Somehow they had heard of me and, with their big company pow wow coming up, were looking for someone with a track record to help them "become more innovative."

Never having heard of them, I Googled their name and, 1.73 seconds later, found myself on their website, slickly designed, I imagined, by someone with a special fondness for iStock photos of earnest looking models impersonating business people. Models, I suspected, who had just moved to L.A. to pursue acting careers, but found themselves working part-time as waiters and jumping at the chance to make some easy money wearing a suit and a smile for a day.

Easy for me to say – me being the proverbial pot calling the proverbial kettle black with my big ass mortgage, family to support and young entrepreneur's dream of making it big so I'd actually have enough money to invest with a financial services firm one day.

My first call with the client was pleasant enough. They talked. I listened, choosing not to interrupt them each time they made their point with an acronym I probably should have known if I only I hadn't spent my young adult years living as a hippie, poet, and monk.

OK, so they weren't a solar energy company. So they weren't asking me to help them end AIDS. I got it. *This was business.* The *money* business. The *big* money business and I was in it, no matter how much Rilke and Rumi I read on the side. Money. This was about money. Money and the VP of something or other inviting me to meet with him and his team on the 57th floor of a building on Wall Street.

Was I thrilled? No. But this was a possible gig and I needed the bread, so I went.

The VP and his team looked nothing like the iStock photos on their company's homepage, though they did have a nice view of Manhattan and a big conference table.

Our conversation went well enough. I asked all the right questions. They gave all the right answers. They sprinkled the conversation with football metaphors. I nodded. They gave me their business cards. I gave them mine. But on the way home, I began to feel a creeping sense of dread, like I was auditioning for a movie I didn't want to be in, a movie being produced by a very fat man, sitting poolside, cell phone and martini in hand.

When they called me back for a third meeting, I was betwixt and between. Do I trust my instincts and tell them I'm not their man? Or do I let go of my judgments and focus on the *possibility* that I might be able to help them get to higher ground?

Eternally the optimist, I chose the latter and decided to meet with them a third time – a meeting, sad to say, which only confirmed that I didn't like them very much and didn't like myself for sitting in a room with them. How could I consider enabling their collective hallucination of themselves as a service organization when all they really wanted to do was make more money?

More chit chat. More coffee. More run it up the flagpole platitudes that littered our conversation like hidden charges on a credit card bill.

This was the moment of truth. My client-to-be cut to the chase and asked me to quote him a fee.

The honorable thing to do would have sounded like "John, I wish you the best of luck, but after deep consideration, I don't think I'm the best possible fit for your company's needs."

But since I hadn't yet mastered the art of speaking my truth, I took the easy way out and *doubled* my fees, expecting they would be so ridiculously high it would be the client's decision to end the relationship, not mine.

"That sounds about right," the client exclaimed, extending his right hand to seal the deal.

Fast forward six weeks later.

It's 8:30 a.m. and I'm on stage in the Oakwood Room on a beautiful island off the coast of Florida. Looking out at the audience, I notice that four of the gathered troops are sleeping, heads on the table. Someone in the front row explains to me that last night had been a "late one" and they'd all stayed up drinking until 4:00 a.m.

I tap the mic and began speaking, trusting that the sound of my amplified voice would be enough to wake the dead. Two of them snap to attention. The other two don't.

I signal the people sitting next to their sleep-deprived peers to poke them, which they do, shooting glances at me as if I was a substitute teacher.

This was, as far I could tell, not a leadership offsite at all, but a college fraternity weekend – big men on campus with stock options, golf shirts, and a very high opinion of themselves. Nothing I say lands. Nothing. Nada. Zilch. Only one thing is clear – I am the highly paid *warm up act* before another night of drinking – a small box they can check off to prove they have done "the innovation thing."

I may have missed the moment of truth back at my client's office weeks ago, but I was not going to miss it today.

"Ladies and gentlemen," I announce. "It's obvious that some of you don't want to be here today. I'm guessing you'd rather be golfing, napping, or checking your email. So... we're going to take a 20-minute break. Only return if you really want to be here. Otherwise, you'll just be dead weight, screwing it up for the rest of us. Kapish?"

Twenty minutes pass. Everyone returns.

And while the rest of the day didn't exactly qualify as one of the great moments in the history of leadership off sites, it wasn't a total loss. Some good things happened. People woke up. People shaped up. People stepped up. And I learned a valuable lesson that would serve me for the rest of my life: *Follow my feeling, not the money trail.*

So What?

Every day we have a choice to play the "world game" with as much integrity as possible. On one hand, we all have mouths to feed (including our own), and this fact sometimes requires compromise. On the other hand, we have five fingers and all of them are pointing at the flaws of corporations across the world and why they don't deserve our help. Ultimately, only you can decide what's the right move to make, "rightness" being highly subjective. If your values are well-defined and your mind is clear, the choice will not be difficult.

Now What?

Consider the choices before you – projects you've been invited into by others who value your services. If any of them feel questionable, out of integrity, or just plain wrong, pause for a moment and reflect. You do not have to say YES. You can say NO. The choice is yours.

THE WEDDING ANNOUNCEMENT

A fter I got fired from my job as a political speechwriter, I found myself in a bind. With an expensive rent to pay on Manhattan's Upper West Side, bills up the wazoo, and no savings to speak of, I knew I had to find another source of income. I had a no clue what that was going to be. The thought of perking up my resume and going out on job interviews was completely unappealing. And the prospect of looking through the want ads was second only to waiting on line at the Department of Motor Vehicles on my list of worst possible ways to spend a day. While there were hundreds of jobs to select from in *The New York Times*, I was very clear I did not want to become a bread delivery man, welder, telemarketer, manufacturer's rep, bus boy, elevator operator, factory worker, security guard, filing clerk, or carpenter's helper.

Obviously, I would have to create my own job. But how? I didn't have a website. I didn't have a business card. And I didn't have any real connections. All I had was an idea – the idea to *declare* myself to the world.

When I thought about what my declaration might look like, the only image that came to mind was *marriage* – not that my job was going to have anything to do with weddings or marrying a wealthy woman. Marriage was just a metaphor, a thought starter for the kind of communication strategy it would take to get the word out – the kind of "declare-it-to-the-world" message that couples in love put out there when it's time to tie the knot.

So that's what I decided to do. I took the following copy to my local print shop and, choosing the finest wedding invitation card stock I could afford, let it rip:

"Mitchell Lewis Ditkoff is happy to announce he is now available for freelance writing in the following areas: speechwriting, advertising copy, brochures, magazine articles, training manuals, scripts, and short stories."

The next day I hand-lettered 100 envelopes and dropped them in a mailbox.

Two days went by. Then a third. Then a fourth, fifth, and sixth. On the seventh day I got my first call – not from the head of a deep-pocketed corporation, but from a New York City spoon-bender, a New Age woman gearing up to promote her mind over matter seminars. Her offer? $25 an hour, plus free attendance to any of her spoon-bending classes. Since most of my spoons were already bent and $25 an hour was not quite what I had in mind, I declined.

The next day I got another call – this time from a recently retired senior executive at AT&T – a well-respected VP of a major business unit who was just about to go on a national speaking tour and needed a speech. He was all business on the phone.

"When are you available to sit down and talk turkey?" he asked.

"Any time this week is good for me," I replied.

"Excellent!" he said. "Let's meet at 7 a.m. tomorrow at your place."

The meeting was good and so was the chemistry. He had a firm handshake, nice shoes, and a pressing need for my services.

"What's your day rate?" he asked.

"$650," I replied, making it up on the spot.

He paused and looked at the ceiling. "Well, since it looks like this project's going to be a multi-week deal, I'm wondering what your package price is."

I paused and also looked at the ceiling.

"How does $600 a day sound?" (more money than I made in a week at the job I'd just lost).

"Sounds good to me," he said. "You've got a deal."

So What?

I'm sure you've heard the expression, "When one door closes, another opens." And the reason you've heard it so much is because it's true. In physics, it is also known as Newton's Third Law of Motion: "For every action, there is an equal and opposite reaction." An earlier version of this principle was articulated in 1756, by the French chemist, Antoine Lavosier, who came up with the law of Conversation of Energy, known to most of us as "Nothing can be created or destroyed, only transformed." Get the picture? Both physically and metaphysically, there is a very cool energetic thing going on in the universe and this very cool thing has great applicability to all of our lives – our social life, our financial life, and our work life. When one door closes, another door opens. Or maybe it's a window...or a mind... or a crack in time in space. One door closing does not signify the end of the world, just a shift in the way that world might look at that moment in time. So, be happy when a door closes. Maybe you actually want the door to close, but don't have the courage to close it yourself. Maybe there is some kind of invisible hand periodically closing doors in your life. Or maybe you just screwed up and a not-very-divine hand has closed the door. Like that idiot from HR. Or your neurotic boss. No matter. Whatever the reason, the closing of a door signals a brand new opportunity and the beginning of the adventure of discovering where the next open door is.

Now What?

Take a few minutes now to think about a door that has recently closed for you – a job lost, an opportunity gone up in smoke, or the end of a relationship. While it may not feel good to think about it, understand that somewhere, "out there," even as you are reading this, another door is opening. Any clues where that door might be and what you can do to knock on it?

Big Blues from the Viagra People

In 1999, I conceived and co-founded the world's first interactive business blues band, Face the Music. The concept was a simple one: to help organizations increase teamwork and decrease complaint by gathering employees into small groups to write and perform original blues songs. The concept resonated with a lot of industries, especially Big Pharma. So we weren't all that surprised when Pfizer came calling. They had a big event coming up and wanted to do "something different" to engage participants – high ranking business leaders from around the world.

Though our approach seemed risky to them at first, our testimonials from other Fortune 500 companies were proof enough that we were the real deal and they happily signed on the dotted line.

Unlike most business simulations, our service began long before we took the stage. Weeks before a gig, we'd interview each client to learn about their frustrations, then write a custom blues song – a kind of musical caricature of their company that we'd perform to kick off their event. And though we routinely shared our lyrics with clients before each event, rarely were we asked to *modify* the songs.

Pfizer was a different story. From their perspective, our lyrics were politically incorrect, incendiary, and "might be taken the wrong way."

Not wanting to blow a big pay day, we revised our lyrics overnight and submitted version 2.0 first thing the next morning.

Pfizer didn't like our new version either. Nor did they like version 3.0, 4.0, or 5.0. After five failed attempts, we decided to drop the custom song and focus all of our attention on the *classic blues songs* that made up the rest of our play list.

But now, doubt had crept into our client's mind. He was officially nervous and wanted to see the lyrics to *all* of our songs.

"Piece of cake," we said to ourselves. The lyrics we'd be sending him had been performed for more than a hundred years and were part of the DNA of America. True. But they weren't part of *Pfizer's* DNA and our client had issues with every song we sent.

So we emailed the lyrics to *another* ten classic blues songs. He rejected those, too.

Now, *we* had the blues. Like the legendary blues musician, Robert Johnson, we stood at the crossroads.

"Gentlemen," I began the conference call in the most corporate voice I could muster, "with all due respect, you have just rejected the lyrics of the most popular 20 American blues songs from the past hundred years. Remember, you are engaging the services of a *blues band*, not a polka band. You've got to have more trust in us."

They hemmed. They hawed. Them hemmed again. And then with a semi-shrug of their collective shoulders, they chose the seven tamest songs and gave us a tepid thumbs up.

"But remember," they warned, "the show has to end no later than 9:30 p.m. sharp. Not a minute more!"

Though outwardly our client greeted us pleasantly enough when we got to the venue, something was off. Inwardly, he was anxious, uptight, frowning, constricted, nervous, and obsessing about how he was going to cover his ass should his worst nightmare come to pass. The band picks up on his mood and immediately tightens up.

Knowing that good music doesn't issue forth from tight musicians, I send the band backstage for a glass of wine while I filibuster with the client, the theater rapidly filling with hundreds of senior executives.

"Remember," the client reminds me as the lights went down, "the show must end at 9:30 sharp. Not a minute later."

The band's first two songs are lame. Uptight from their contact with the client backstage, they are playing it safe, not exactly a formula for foot stomping blues. By the third song, thank God, they find their groove. The audience relaxes and the songs are a hoot. Everyone is having a great time.

Then I look at my watch. It is 9:27. I signal the band to wrap things up when, out of the corner of my eye, I see the client making his way to the stage. Actually, "making his way" wasn't the phrase to describe his approach. "Storming the stage" was more like it. I look at my watch again. Now it is 9:28. I speak faster, doing my best to finish before the bewitching hour. Two sentences from closure, the man bounds up the stairs and lunges in my direction.

"*KEEP PLAYING!*" he blurts. "*Tell the band to keep playing!!* This is *really* going well! Forget the 9:30 deadline. *Keep playing!*"

The band segues into B.B. King's "Let the Good Times Roll." *South Side Denny* takes off on a blistering guitar solo, *South Side Slim* wails at the top of his lungs. *Screaming Sweet Pea Fradon* brings down the house. *Blind Lemon Pledge* is on top of his game. Everyone in the audience is singing and dancing and clapping and laughing. The pharmaceutical blues? Gone. At least for the moment.

So What?

Some people say that laughter is the universal language. Some say love. I say complaint – at least in today's business world. No matter what industry, country, or culture, bitching and moaning tend to rule the day. If you have any doubt, consider this: according to a recent study, 62% of all American workers consider themselves dissatisfied with work. Unfortunately, most organizations have learned to live with complaint. But complaint

– unacknowledged, unaddressed, and unresolved – is more than just an irritant. It's bad business – the proverbial elephant in the room – an untrained and smelly one, at that.

Even the best run organizations have no clue how to deal with complaint. Oh sure, for their *customers* they have a "complaint department," but for their *employees*, not much more is offered than an occasional workforce survey – all too often a useless exercise in quantifying what everyone already knows.

The Pfizer leader who engaged our services understood this phenomenon. At least *theoretically*. But when it came time to trusting the process, all bets were off. Alas, it is this lack of trust that is often the root cause of complaint in any corporation. When employees are not trusted, they don't feel empowered, and when they don't feel empowered, they become resigned, and when they become resigned they either *resign* (costing the company thousands of dollars to retrain their replacements) or they *retract*, further feeding the complaint monster.

The paradox? The very resource Pfizer brought in to help them restore trust was, itself, not trusted. The silver lining? We were able to go beyond our own brand of business blues and adapt to the needs of the moment. We were able to perform at a high level even when being micromanaged by a man who probably thought John Lee Hooker had something to do with "the world's oldest profession." We could have complained, but we didn't, choosing instead to transmute our client's request for a blues song that didn't "stir things up" into music that healed – providing an opportunity for 100 head honchos to give voice to their angst and deepen their focus on what they were originally hired to do – provide humanity with medicines that helped restore health and well-being.

NOW WHAT?

What is your biggest complaint at work these days? What is the biggest complaint of the team you work most closely with? And what can you do, in the next 30 days, to quicken the process of going beyond these business blues?

THE DATE NIGHT BLUES

The roots of the blues go all the way back to Africa, winding their way through centuries worth of hurt and betrayal, then surfacing again in the early 20th century in North America. Here, sharecroppers, men on chain gangs, and other disenfranchised souls did their best to ease their pain by giving voice to what ailed them.

Much has been written about the blues, most notably by W.C. Handy. But what hasn't been written about much is one of the modern day correlatives – the roots of the blues for new parents.

The blues of new parents go all the back to the first six months after the birth of their first child. As the intoxication (and gift certificates) of new parenthood wears off and the harsh realities of diaper change, sleep deprivation, and less frequent sex wears on, most couples find their relationship standing at the crossroads of funky and frayed.

The traditional way most parents deal with this phenomenon is known in the literature as "date night" – that sacred, once-a-week, get-out-of-the-house escapade to focus on something other than baby food or obsessive thoughts about the rising costs of college.

My wife and I were no exception. Date Night for us, however, soon became synonymous with *Movie Night* and *Movie Night* soon became synonymous with *Same Old, Same Old* night, which, unfortunately, left both of us feeling even crankier than ever.

Aware of the rut we were in, I decided to step up my game and do something different, which, in our case, meant checking out the entertainment section of the *Woodstock Times*.

And there, on page three, as plain as the milk mustache on my young son's face, I saw it – a small ad for Ernie and the Wildcats, a local blues band I had never heard of playing at a local blues club I had never heard of. Bingo! The blues it was! Who cared that these guys had never opened for B.B. King? At least they weren't a movie at the 12-Plex.

One appetizer, two margaritas, and three blues songs later, Date Night 2.0 had not only revived our spirits, it had morphed into *Ideate Night*, that curious parting of the cerebral Red Sea when a new possibility makes itself known. Halfway through Stormy Monday, I had one of those moments.

My realization? *All my clients had the blues!* But what they didn't have was a healthy way to go *beyond* the blues. And because they didn't, complaint ruled the day – complaint and all his funky, low-down, younger cousins: bitching, moaning, griping, and kvetching.

The idea at the root of this realization? To provide my clients with a cool way to identify their blues, form ad hoc blues bands, write work-related blues songs, then perform their songs for their fellow corporate sharecroppers.

I logged on this morning
And found out I'd been spammed,
Got 500 emails, Lord, my inbox was way too jammed,
Most of it was useless, the rest of it was jokes,
Sent by friends with downtime to the rest of us working folks.

The first thing I did the next morning was share my breakthrough with my two best friends. They were not impressed. Neither were they interested, intrigued, astounded, amazed, fascinated, congratulatory, or wanting to get in on the ground floor. They thought I'd lost my mind.

Unperturbed, I shared the idea with another friend – a creative, bass-playing OD consultant with a penchant for the unusual. His eyes opened wide as he told me how he and his brothers used to do something similar at parties. Paul was in!

The next day, we pitched partner #3, a talented, keyboard-playing carpenter from Dublin. He was in, too. A month of late night, brainstorming sessions later and the three of us had the beta version of Face the Music and nailed our first client, GE. Two months later, *Fast Company* ran a story on us. Three months after that, CNN filmed one of our gigs and had it playing in steady rotation worldwide.

SO WHAT?

Breakthrough ideas can show up anywhere, anytime, anyhow – and they *do*, especially after extended periods of frustration, confusion, and doubt – when the 9-5 conscious mind (assuming it's committed to finding a better way) gives way to the 24/7 subconscious mind – the unheralded, underground, little-known genius problem-solver we all have who loves nothing better than conjuring up extraordinary solutions in the 11th hour. The conditions, for me, that night, at my local blues club, were ideal for originating a big idea. I had a big need, the urge to do something different, and the recognition that I couldn't do it all myself. And now? That late night, date-night, at-the-crossroads idea has spawned more than a thousand business blues songs and a major renaissance of truth telling and teamwork in organizations worldwide.

NOW WHAT?

What are you frustrated about these days at work? What's not working the way you want it to? And what can you do to put yourself in a place where brilliance, insights, and breakthrough ideas are just waiting to be discovered?

THE OPTIC FIBER HECKLER

Every person who has ever had a job has experienced at least one moment of truth in their work life – a time when all the chips were on the table and the decision of whether to go "all in" had to be made. One such moment happened to me when I was facilitating an innovation workshop for 110 of Lucent Technology's "best and brightest" – a room full of brilliant computer scientists and engineers with more Ph.D.s than most politicians have excuses.

There I was, on stage, introducing my session with a Power Point show of quotes from legendary innovators, when a man in the tenth row stood up and screamed, "You are totally wrong! I used to work with that guy and he *never* would have said anything like that! If you can't get your quotes straight, why should I believe *anything* you're about to tell us?"

If this was the Wild West, I had just been challenged to a duel at high noon, armed only with a remote and a blueberry muffin.

Standing as I was in the epicenter of the optic fiber universe, I had only a few seconds to assess the situation. There was no time for a strategic plan, no time for deliberation, no time to call my coach. This was Defcon 1.

"Well," I began (stalling for as much time as a single word would allow), "it is possible that you are correct. The slides I'm showing today were just finalized yesterday and my assistant may have made an incorrect attribution. I will check with her when I get back to the office. That being said, I invite you to focus on the *good stuff* that's here for you today, not the possible flaws."

Logical? Yes. Effective? No. My comments only made my antagonist angrier, his face growing redder by the moment.

Now I had a choice to make – whether to further engage my corporate heckler in a heroic attempt to win him over, or continue with the reason why I was hired in the first place – to help predominantly left-brained technologists tap into their slightly atrophied right brains.

Choosing Door #2, I proceed to teach a powerful creative thinking technique based on the thinking styles of Albert Einstein and Garry Kasparov (a former Soviet Union Grand Chess Master).

Technique taught, I move off to one side of the stage in an attempt to make myself as invisible as possible and allow the audience to focus on the task at hand. For the next five minutes, everything goes smoothly, each of the Lucent scientists applying the technique to their most pressing business challenges.

Then, without warning, Mr. You-Got-Your-Slides-All-Wrong stands up and, with great velocity, begins approaching the stage. On a scale of 1-10, with "1" being *walking* and "10" being *storming*, he is a 9.8.

The faster he walks, the quieter the room gets as I take my stance and, as a practicing martial artist, ready myself for whatever was going to happen next. Two feet from me, he stops, eyes on fire, and begins to speak.

"This is amazing!" he exclaims.

"What is amazing?" I reply.

"The technique you just taught," he explains. "I've just had an incredible breakthrough – something I've been struggling with for the past three years!"

I do not have to duck. I do not have to block, I do not have to kick – only *listen*, as the man standing before me goes on and on about his new idea and how it is going to change the game – for him, his team, and, lo, I say I unto you, for his entire organization.

Happy for him and greatly relieved, I acknowledge his breakthrough and ask if he'd be willing share it with the group – a task that would require the two of us to change roles – him taking center stage as *teacher* and me taking his seat, as *student*. Which is exactly what we do.

I couldn't have asked for a better spokesperson for the message I was trying to convey that day – about the innate ability all human beings have to go beyond their limiting assumptions and enter into the realm where breakthrough insights abide. My heckler's dramatic and very visible shift from left-brained naysaying to right-brained curiosity embodied a teaching I couldn't have scripted in a hundred years.

So What?

None of us know when the moment of truth will come. None of us know what it will look like and how we will respond. But we do know this: if you are alive and engaged in your work, it will come. The more you are "all in," the easier it will be for you to respond to whatever comes your way.

My moment of confrontation at Lucent did not allow me the luxury of deep deliberation. I had to trust myself to go with the flow. But even more than that, I had to be willing to reframe what seemed to be a *problem* into an *opportunity*. I had to make lemonade out of lemons without squirting any in the eyes of those I was there to serve. My task was not to find fault with the fault-finder but to transform the moment into deeper understanding.

On the front lines of business, it is very easy to find fault in others. Even on a good day, most of us are woefully imperfect – filled with a lifetime's worth of quirks, projections, fears, habits, and routines – the kind of stuff that bugs even our closest friends. Throw in the X factor of stress, heavy workloads, constantly changing priorities, and you have a formula for... well... major heckling.

Your mission, should you choose to accept this assignment, is *not to take it personally.* The person who is heckling you is most likely having a bad day, week, month, quarter, year, or life. You just happen to be a convenient excuse for your company's resident hecklers to let off steam. If you react with the same negativity that comes toward you you'll only end up throwing fuel on the fire. If you hate being judged, but judge the judgers for judging, you will get lost in a funhouse hall of mirrors with no exit.

P.S. At lunch, after my workshop at Lucent my client informed me of three things:

1) The man who heckled me did the same thing to *every* outside speaker; 2) The exchange between the heckler and me was the perfect embodiment of one of Lucent's core values – *allowing creative dissonance,* and 3) As a result of my session's positive impact, Lucent committed to licensing my company's creative thinking training. Lemons hadn't just turned into lemonade, they'd turned into some major cash flow, too.

NOW WHAT?

Think of a moment of truth that you've experienced during the past year, a surprise encounter that demanded an intuitive response. What was it like for you? What did you learn? And, if your response did not work, what might you do differently next time?

GIVE ME THE MONEY
OR I'LL BLOW YOUR FUCKING HEAD OFF

Three o'clock in the morning is not my favorite time of day. Too early to be late and too late to be early, it's a nether world, a place not to linger. Kind of like puberty.

It was this time of the day/night where I found myself at the Homestead Motor Inn, five months into my tour of duty as the long-haired night desk clerk. The bar had just closed and I was attending to some routine administrative tasks when a very forgettable looking man made his way across the lobby, handed me a $5.00 bill and asked me for change. I gave him four singles and four quarters, sat down on my chair, back to the lobby, and returned to reading my book. Two minutes passed.

"Oh, one more thing, buddy," I hear the now familiar voice ask.

When I turn around, he isn't all that forgettable looking anymore. He's pointing a gun at my head, beckoning me with his left hand to come closer.

"Give me the money," he demands, "or I'll blow your fucking head off."

Like a bit actor in a direct-to-video movie, I make my way to the cash register and pull out the bills.

"Now get out from behind the desk," he demands, signaling me to walk with him, across the lobby, to the men's room.

"Get in!" he says, pushing the door open. "And stay there!"

"How long should I stay?" I ask.

"Five minutes!" he barks, and with that, he is gone.

I really didn't need to go to the bathroom, but since I'm here, I figure, what the hell, so I walk to the urinal and take a leak. I look at my watch, wondering if five minutes is up, when it dawns on me that the guy who just held me up is not waiting outside the bathroom door and timing me.

So I exit and call the cops. They arrive in five minutes, grill me for 20, dust for fingerprints, and exit stage left, telling me "they will be in touch."

Two days pass – two days to think about what might have happened, but didn't. The good news? The odds of it happening again were, statistically speaking, close to zero. The way I figured it, I had somehow, gotten this "hold up thing" out of my system and could get on with my life.

So there I am behind the front desk just 48 hours later when another forgettable looking man walks across the lobby. But he does not ask for change. He just puts a gun to my head and repeats the mantra of the week. "Give me the money or I'll blow your fucking ahead off."

This guy, however, is not nearly as smooth as the first guy. His hands are shaking. He's sweating and has a nervous look in his eye.

A professional victim by now, I know the drill, so I walk to the cash register, give him the money, and walk myself to the men's room. I pee again, wait two minutes, not five, then call the cops. Again they arrive quickly, only this time they relate to me very differently than before.

You see, the Homestead Motor Inn hadn't been held up in five years. Now, two out of three nights, it's been robbed and I am the only eyewitness – me, the long-haired, new-in-town, anti-establishment desk clerk. Things weren't looking good for me.

The avuncular Detective Wallace puts his arm around my shoulder and asks me to *confess*, explaining how he understands how tough it must be for someone like me, being so new in town, to be living on such meager wages.

"But… I… didn't do it," I say.

That's when the second detective steps forward.

"Mitch, since this would be your first offense, things will go easy for you. Just tell us what you did."

"Like I said, Detective, I didn't do it. I'm not your thief."

But the two men of the law are not convinced. And the more I proclaim my innocence, the more they start seeing holes in my story.

The more they treat me like the thief, the more guilty I feel – a mix of knowing I *could* have done it and how I usually feel when going through airport security and nothing beeps – even though I know I must have something beepable on me.

"Here's the deal, Mitch," they explain. "Tomorrow morning we want you to come down to the stationhouse and look through some mug shots. You know, to see if you can find these guys, eh?"

So the next morning, I find myself turning page after page of mug shots, bad-ass-looking criminals staring me in the face. The first book yields nothing. But the halfway through the second, I see him, the second guy, the nervous guy. It was him!

"Are you sure it's him?" ask the cops. "Are you sure?"

"Well," I say, looking again. "I'm 99% sure."

Neither of the detectives are pleased. "You can't be 99% sure. You've gotta be 100% sure. The judge will throw us out of court if you're only 99% sure."

The guy I pointed out, explain the cops, was your basic two-time loser. He had gotten out of jail three months before and was working in a home for the mentally disabled just a few miles away. If it wasn't me who had robbed the hotel, they reasoned, it had to be him.

"Just say the word," they tell me, "and we'll lock this guy away for ten years."

"Like I said, Detective, I'm 99% sure. I mean the whole thing happened so fast."

"OK, we get it, son. Here's what we're gonna do. Tomorrow, we're gonna drive you down to his place of business and we're gonna walk him by you, nice and slow. If it's him, all you gotta do is nod. Kapish? Just nod. See you at 2:00 p.m.."

I didn't sleep well that night. The scene had definitely changed. No longer was I a bit player in a B movie, I was now starring in a Kafka novel.

The ride to the Home for the Mentally Disabled was not what I would call a joy ride. I sat in the backseat attempting to appear as innocent as possible. The cops sat in the front seat drinking coffee. When we arrive, they walk me down a long, tiled hallway and sit me down on a hard wooden bench.

"OK, buddy. In a few minutes, we're gonna walk this creep right by you. If it's him, all you gotta do is nod. That's it, nod. We'll take it from there."

I can see by the way the "creep" is walking down the hallway that he is attempting a very different kind of gait than the guy who held me up. It was, shall we say, a casual gait, a "I-think-I'll-get-a-Twinkie-out-of-the-vending-machine gait" – not a "Give-me-the-money-or-I'll-blow-your-fucking-head-off gait" – his version of the way I'd been sitting in the backseat of the squad car just a few minutes ago.

The cops stare at me, waiting for the nod.

"Is it him?" they ask.

"Well," I reply, "it sure looks a lot like him. I'm…like… 99% sure it's him."

Now the cops are really pissed.

"OK, Mr. Can't-Make-Up-His-Mind." Here's what we're gonna do. We're gonna sit this guy down in the room across the hall and we're gonna interrogate him. While that's happening, you walk up to the door, look through the window, and get a good, long look. If it's him, all you gotta do is nod."

A few minutes go by as the detectives set the scene. I walk to the window and look in just as I've been instructed. The guy looks a lot like the guy who held me up. He has a lot of the same features. I mean, he could be this guy's fraternal twin, but am I 100% sure? No. And I tell the cops so, which is not what they want to hear.

"OK, young man, we're going to give you one last chance. You stand here. Don't move. We're going to walk this guy up the hallway so the two of you will be face to face. Just you and him. Don't worry, we'll be standing close by. Nothing bad is going to happen to you. All you need to do is look him in the eye and nod if it's him."

So there we are, the two of us – him, the two-time loser mopping floors for a living and me, the long-haired night desk clerk with not a single eyewitness on his side.

He stares at me and I stare at him.

"Hello, again," I say in my mind.

"Shit!" I hear him think. "Have mercy on me, man. It was only 800 bucks."

"But dude," I think, "robbing people isn't cool. Somebody could get hurt."

From behind me, I hear a voice. "So, Mitch? Is it him?"

"Like I said before, Detective. I'm 99% sure. But I'm not 100% sure."

So What?

This story has baffled me for years – not so much for the specifics of what happened, but what I made of what happened. On different days, I interpret this story in different ways. The logical, law-abiding part of me believes the guy I picked out of the mug shot book was the guy who held me up. The long-haired, anti-establishment 22-year-old part of me still isn't sure. And, of course, there's another wrinkle to the story – my telepathic moment in the hallway and the request for mercy from the man standing before me. Bottom line, I don't know and will never know what the "right" thing to do was – just like you don't know whether the conclusions you've drawn from the stories in your life are anything more than your perceptions, projections, assumptions, and beliefs based on the circumstantial evidence of the moment and the curious way you happen to connect the dots.

Now What?

Think of a challenging encounter you've had in your life – a divorce, accident, mistake, fight, missed opportunity, failure, or big disappointment – an incident that could have been interpreted in more than one way. Now see this incident through the eyes of the other person – someone with a totally different point of view. What story would they tell?

I WANT MY MTV

A nyone who owns a business, whether they've been to business school or not, knows one thing: You need customers. No customers, no business. *How* you get customers, of course, is the question.

In my business, one of the main ways to get business is responding to RFPs – requests for proposals. Here's how it works: a company hears about you, checks out your website, contacts you, schedules a call, tries to figure out if you're the real deal, and, if you pass their sniff test, they ask you to submit a proposal.

In the beginning of my career, I would get very excited whenever anyone asked me to submit an RFP. It meant I had a big one on the line, a horse in the race, my hat in the ring, or whatever other metaphor I could conjure up to reinforce my belief that I was actually going to make a living. Like a beanie-wearing college freshman, I dove into the proposal writing process with great zeal.

In time, however, responding to RFPs made me very cranky. I came to learn that only one in ten proposals would make the grade and that the other nine, which I had so diligently crafted, were merely my response to bogus fishing expeditions from the client. Either they had already decided on their vendor, were testing the waters, wanted free insights, or were merely hunting for the low-cost provider.

So when MTV Networks called, I was betwixt and between. Do I play the game and spend the better part of my day writing a proposal or do I walk my talk and do something different?

Since I'd already done some work for MTV, I decided the time was right to experiment, so I asked myself a question: "How can I radically reduce the time it takes me to write a proposal that gets results?" The answer came quickly – the TWO WORD proposal. In 200 point type, I wrote the words "TRUST US" with an asterisk after the second "S" – and, at the bottom of the page, in 8-point type, noted our fee. That was it. Two words and a bottom line.

On the day my proposal is due, I walk into the office of MTV's CFO. After the ritual chitchat and cup of coffee, he asks me if I had the proposal.

"Yes, I do, Jim. But first let me ask you a question. Do you get a lot of proposals?"

He laughs, pointing to a huge stack on his desk.

"And do you like reading proposals?"

Jim looks at me as if I had just asked if he liked sticking forks in his eyes.

"Good!" I say, "then there's a good chance you will love my proposal. But in order to give it to you, I need to get further away."

And with that warning, I begin backing away. When I get as far away as possible, I stop and hold my proposal in the air for him to see.

Even from across the room, Jim can read my two words: TRUST US!

Smiling, he beckons me forward, takes the proposal from my hands, lowers his eyes to the bottom line, and extends his hand.

"You've got a deal," he says.

Two words in big bold type and a bottom line. That's all it took. Two minutes. Not two hours.

So What?

"We have approximately 60,000 thoughts in a day," said Deepak Chopra. "Unfortunately, 95 percent of them are thoughts we had the day before." That's how most human beings roll. Creatures of habit, we find a groove and stay in it until it becomes a rut. Then it runs so deep, we have a hard time getting out, and so we decorate our walls with Dilbert cartoons and pictures of our last vacation. Sometimes, we need to do something different. Will this "something different" work every time? No, it won't. But it will work sometimes. My two-word proposal was the perfect thing for MTV. It wouldn't have been the perfect thing for a new client or the IRS, but for MTV it got the job done.

NOW WHAT?

Think of a proposal, pitch, or presentation you need to make in the next few weeks. On one side of a piece of paper, write down all the reasonable things you can do to get the gig. Then, on the flip side, write down all the unreasonable things – new approaches, new ideas, and new ways to make your case. After you write your first wave of unreasonable approaches, write your second wave. Then pick one and go for it.

The Awesome Power of Immersion

"If I had an hour to solve a problem," explained Albert Einstein, "I'd spend the first 55 minutes thinking about the problem, and the last five solving it."

Translation? One of the secrets to having a breakthrough is immersion – *"the state of being deeply engaged, involved, or absorbed."*

Immersion is the ocean in which our insights, ideas, and illuminations are swimming. That's why yogis seek out caves, embryos gestate, and writers go on retreat.

And that's why my business partner and I rented a townhouse in Boulder, Colorado for 30 days and 30 nights when it was time for us to start our company. We knew we had a great idea for a business, but we also knew that ideas were a dime a dozen and that unless we *immersed* ourselves we'd end up with nothing much more than a charming story to tell at cocktail parties.

Armed with little more than a flipchart, a few marking pens, and a burning desire to create something new, we unplugged from all our other commitments and jumped in with both feet.

We talked. We walked. We walked our talk. We noodled, conjured, brainstormed, blue-skied, read, sang, stretched, drank coffee, wine, enjoyed the crisp Colorado air, and whatever else it took to free ourselves from the gravity of what we already knew. If this was Rocky 1, our townhouse was the gym, Adrienne nowhere in sight. And every night before we went to bed, we'd remind each other to remember our dreams and speak them aloud the first thing in the morning. Clues. We were looking for clues, hints, perfumed handkerchiefs dropped by our muse while we slept, and anything else that bubbled to the surface of the vast imaginal stew we found ourselves now swimming in.

Crackpots? No. More like *crockpots*, simmering in our own creative juices, unimpaired by the almost infinite number of distractions we'd grown accustomed to calling our lives. The walls of our abode? Covered with paper, sketches, scribbles, Post-its®, quotes, pictures, lists, charts, diagrams, questions, and take out menus – the barely decipherable hieroglyphics of our journey into the unknown.

But our immersion went far beyond the walls of our abode. It was a state of mind, not a geographical location. It didn't matter where we were. Walking by the creek or sitting in a bar was all the same to us, ruled as we were by our shared fascination, random bits of conversation with strangers, and the increasingly apparent sense that we were on to something big.

And then, on the morning of the 19th day, there was a knock on the door – a loud and insistent knock, a knock both of us found odd since nobody knew where we lived – or so we thought.

"It's open," Steven shouted from across the room. "Let yourself in."

There, at the threshold, stood a woman neither of us knew, a woman boldly announcing that, for the past three days, she'd been hearing about "these two creativity guys" she just had to meet, her business now on the cusp of either breaking through or breaking down.

I don't remember a single thing we said to her, but whatever it was hit the nail on the head.

The next day, there was another knock on the door. Apparently, someone else had heard about our whereabouts. This guy had a business, too, or was *trying* to have a business. He spoke. We listened. He spoke some more. We listened some more, occasionally asking a question and sharing some insight. He, too, got what he needed.

On the third day, Jesus did not rise from the grave, but, yes, there was another knock on the door – just enough proof to the logical part of our minds that the previous two visits were not random events, but part of some kind of emerging pattern – what fans of Rupert Sheldrake might refer to as manifestations of the morphogenetic field or what less metaphysical folks might describe as our very own "field of dreams."

Steven and I had done nothing we knew of to draw these people to us – no ads in the paper, no posters on poles, no calls, no emails, no social marketing campaigns. The only thing we'd done was *immerse* – to dig deeply into our own highly charged process of creating something new. But this "nothing at all" wasn't nothing at all. It was *something* – something grand and glorious.

Is a mother hen sitting on her egg doing nothing at all? Is she slacking? Is her seeming disappearance from the poultry marketplace a sign of irresponsibility?

To the casual observer, maybe that's what it looks like, but nothing could be further from the truth. Sitting is exactly what the mother hen needs to do in order to bring new life into the world. Stillness, not action, is her path.

Did Steven and I accomplish what we set out to do during our 30 days of immersion? Yes, we did. In spades. We emerged with the design of our first product – a creative thinking training we ended up licensing to AT&T just two years later.

Was our immersion all fun and games? No it wasn't. Chaos and confusion were our ever-present housemates, but the rent they paid sparked a ton of learning, discovery, and a willingness to make friends with the unknown – what Henry Miller was referring to when he defined confusion as "simply a word we've invented for an order which is not yet understood."

In today's business world, immersion is a rare commodity. Attention Deficit Disorder rules the day. Time is sliced and diced. We don't have time. Time has us. We tweet, we delete, we tap our feet, but all too often nothing much beyond the status quo ever happens. Downtime has become anathema. *Busy-ness* and *business* have become synonymous. The assumption? The more we do and the faster we do it, the more success we'll have. Boil an egg? Ha! We microwave it – even if it tastes like shit. Dive in? No way. We hydroplane. But it doesn't have to be that way.

Slowing down and going deep trumps speeding up and going crazy. Immersion trumps diversion. It's possible. Yes, it is. I have proof. And so do you, if only you would pause long enough to remember those extraordinary times when you unplugged, tuned in, and dove into your own personal process of conjuring up something wonderful.

So What?

Today's fast-paced world is not set up for immersion. Short and sweet is the name of the game. Twitter is God or, if not God, then at least God's preferred communication platform. But you, oh multi-tracking savant of infinite possibilities, do not have to be sucked up into this vortex of speed. With just a little bit of forethought, you can unplug and immerse, if even for just a day at a time.

Now What?

Take out your smart phone. Click on the calendar icon. Notice the next six months. Now, identify, a day, week, two weeks, or month when you can unplug from the madness and immerse yourself in a project that is important to you. Now enter those dates in your calendar (and set a few alarms).

THE BRILLIANT
COMPLAINT DEPARTMENT

When AT&T was deregulated in 1984, it opened the door for something the organization never had to deal with before – *competition*. No longer a monopoly, Ma Bell became simply another telecommunications company, albeit a big one with lots of benefits to pay and a nice logo.

With upstarts like MCI and Sprint entering the scene, AT&T was quickly discovering that not only was its lunch being eaten, so was its breakfast, dinner, and late night snack.

Clearly, something needed to be done to right the ship and that's why AT&T decided to launch its "WinBack" program, a noble attempt to win back customers who, attracted by MCI and Sprint's promotional offerings, had gone over to the "dark side."

That's when AT&T reached out and called my company.

Their request was a simple one – for us to lead a series of brainstorming sessions that would spark the kind of ideas that would send MCI and Sprint back to the Stone Age – or, at the very least, back to 1958.

For three months, we facilitated a series of ideation sessions for our new, non-monopolistic client. Many ideas were generated. Many cups of coffee were consumed. Many Post-its˚ were posted. But after five sessions, it became obvious that every group was coming up with the same ideas. And while our overlords were perfectly willing to bring us back again and again to spark even more ideas, we could not, in good faith, return without first informing our client of the "same old, same old" syndrome.

It didn't take a genius to figure out why. The groups were all composed of the same kind of people, the "usual suspects," senior leaders with power ties, impressive titles, and enviable parking spaces. Yes, they were smart. Yes, they were experienced. And yes, they were motivated. But they also inhabited the same box, *the box of expertise*. What we needed was a different mix of people. *Unusual suspects*.

"Who else you got?" we asked. "How about the untapped, unappreciated, and under-valued?"

The answer came faster than AT&T's rate increases: *The Complaint Department*, a group of 20 long-term employees whose sole focus was listening to customer gripes – day after kvetchy day.

The profile of the Complaint Department was very different than the profile of AT&T's senior leaders. For starters, they were mostly women – *women of color.* Few of them had a college education. And this was not a group considered to be all that creative. That's why we were thrilled to be working with them. Since no one had ever invited them to a brainstorming session before, they had no bad meeting habits and no preconceived notions of what was possible.

The results were extraordinary. In two days, these fabulous women generated more brilliant ideas to regain AT&T's rapidly dwindling market share than the previous five sessions of senior leaders had generated in the past three months.

So What?

During the past 25 years, I've asked more than 10,000 people where and when they get their best ideas. More than 98% tell me they get their best ideas *outside* of the workplace – early in the morning, late at night, dreaming, exercising, showering, commuting, or any number of other catalytic times and places.

And while there are many reasons why individuals don't get their best ideas at work, there are at least as many reasons why organizations don't – the main one being the tendency to rely on the usual suspects.

The AT&T example is only one of many I've seen. Somehow, even the most forward thinking organizations have become creative elitists, inviting only the usual suspects to their brainstorming sessions, as if great ideas were the logical extension of the "3 E's" – education, experience, and expertise. They're not.

In many ways, education, experience, and expertise are the enemy – tidy little boxes that constrict, confine, and constrain.

Instead of being the springboard to possibility, they become the quicksand.

Why did the kings of old have court jesters on the payroll? Because the court jesters had fresh eyes, were not afraid to speak the truth, and were free of the rules and protocols that drove the other courtiers up the castle walls.

This is the challenge all organizations face – how to access the insight, creativity, and ideas of their biggest capital asset – the untapped brilliance of their workforce – no matter how many degrees, stock options, or parking spaces they have.

NOW WHAT?

Think of a big opportunity before you. On an 8x11 piece of paper, make two columns: 1) Usual Suspects and 2) Unusual Suspects. In the Usual Suspects column, jot down the names of people who have attended past ideation sessions you've organized. In the Unusual Suspects column, jot down the names of people you have never invited – people with different points of view, personality, or experience. Then choose a few of these unusual suspects to invite to your next session.

POACHED EGGS

The Old Stone Bakery and Restaurant in Oak Bluffs, Massachusetts was not what I would call a 5-Star restaurant. Not 4. Not 3. I'm guessing it was somewhere between a 2.3 and a 2.7, depending on the day of the week and how hungry you were. Known more for its fresh baked goods than cuisine, it was the kind of place that tourists went when watching their budgets.

Other than the fact that my good friend, Steve, was the baker, I wouldn't have noticed it. Unemployed, going out to eat was not an option for me. And with Steve returning home at the crack of dawn each day with bags of cookies the size of Frisbees, why did I need to work? God was providing. And besides, working in the summer was against my religion – the First Church of the Long Hang. Working seemed... so... uncool... so boring...

a premature concession to entering the real world, which I was putting off as long as possible.

My girlfriend didn't see it that way. She needed stuff and whatever small amount of money she had saved from her last job was running out. So when Steve returned home after yet another nightshift with news that the cook had quit, my girlfriend saw it as a great opportunity for me to get a job.

"But I don't know how to cook!" I exclaimed. "Other than an occasional omelet and grilled cheese, I'm useless."

But she would have none of it, nor would Steve. And so the next day, I found myself standing face to face with Peter White, the owner of the restaurant.

"Steven tells me you're a cook," he said.

"Yes, I am," I lied.

"Good," he said. "Be here tomorrow, 6:00 a.m."

Steve was tickled. Both of us would now have a chance to eat fresh baked cookies together when his shift ended. My girlfriend was tickled, too, because I was now a working man. I, on the other hand, was not tickled. "Terrified" was more like it. "Shocked" and "paralyzed" were other words that came to mind. In a curious way, I was up for the challenge, but I knew I had some major homework to do in the 14 hours before my shift began.

My girlfriend begins the process by instructing me on the basics: how to cut vegetables, how make a sauce, and how to make soup. I take notes on little scraps of paper, which soon litter the table like a kidnap letter torn into strips.

Four hours later, I am donning my apron and surveying the kitchen of the Old Stone Bakery and Restaurant. The first thing I notice is the stove. It's in full view of the customers. Supposedly, this has something to do with the "charm" of the place, but to me all it means is another big helping of performance anxiety.

The first few orders are a breeze: Cheese omelets, scrambled eggs, and flapjacks. The waitresses are impressed. The customers are pleased. Even I start feeling like I can do this. Then Jenny comes barging into the kitchen and bellows "poached eggs". Poached eggs? *Poached eggs?* I have no clue what poached eggs are.

No time to spare, I turn to one of the waitresses and, in a half whisper, ask, "What the hell are poached eggs?" Amused, she explains not only what they are, but also the fine art of making them – the boiling of the water, the cracking of the egg, the tilting of the egg into the boiling water, the brief immersion, the scooping egg motion, and the plating of the egg. OK. Not rocket science. The first five times I try it, the egg explodes in the water. The sixth time, the same thing. And the seventh. And the eighth. And the ninth. Nine times I try and nine times all I get is a strange, yellow floating hieroglyphic.

This is the moment of truth. So I grab the poached-egg-ordering-waitress by the shoulders, look deep into her eyes and, with all the "don't-get-our-crazy-chef-pissed-off" mojo I can muster, instruct her to tell her customer that *"our chef does not make poached eggs"* – the implication being that there was something hopelessly wrong with the out-of-town-poached-egg-ordering tourist for even considering that kind of bogus request.

Lunch is a breeze. The special? Mediterranean Egg Drop Lemon Soup right out of my now very stained, *Vegetarian Epicure.* It's a huge hit. A week later, one of my regulars makes me one of those white, puffy chef's hats – a kind of papal proclamation of my culinary genius. A week after that customers start asking for my recipes, which gives me the opportunity to exit the kitchen, approach my fans, and, in a very thick Mid-Eastern accent from a mythical country, explain my secret, "How you say, in America, ze limon rind – to be scraping just enough from top of ze lemon."

Six months. I cooked for six months. I learned something new, made a good living, had the time of my life, and never once made a poached egg.

So What?

William Shakespeare said it best: "All the world's a stage, and all the men and women merely players. They have their exits and entrances. And one man in his time plays many parts." My job as a cook was one of those parts. Did I know my lines before I stepped on the stage? No. But I learned them quickly, the challenge all of us face these days. With the speed of life increasing exponentially, each of us must be willing to enter from the wings and wing it. Will it work every time? Of course not. I was making scrambled eggs, not performing brain surgery, so we're not talking life and death here. Still, the *spirit* of what I'm talking about prevails. Step up! Step in! Step on stage and begin!

Now What?

Think of an opportunity before you that you are under-qualified to do. Maybe it's a new job or a project with a high degree of difficulty. While there's probably somebody far more suited to do it than you, guess what? YOU are at the right place at the right time to make a go of it. What can you do this week to learn what you need to learn to give it your best shot?

How Would Santa Do It?

"Necessity," it is said, "is the mother of invention." It is. But it is also the father, aunt, uncle, grandmother, cousin, and in-law. For most of us, unless there is a proverbial fire under our proverbial butts, we remain victims of the status quo. Objects at rest. Bumps on a log. If we're not motivated to change, we don't.

Allow me to be more specific. The year was 1998. Although the U.S. economy was in good shape, my business was not. The pipeline was clogged. The marketing plan was a mess. And our cash flow *wasn't*. Semi-fearless leader that I was, I bought some muffins and called a meeting. It took us all of 20 minutes to realize we had three choices if we wanted to stay in business: cut costs, find new clients, or resurrect old clients.

Cutting costs wasn't an option. Costs were already cut. Finding new clients sounded good, but also sounded like a lot of work. Resurrecting *old* clients, on the other hand, had a nice ring to it. And so we decided to focus our efforts on the local scene – companies who had bought from us before and were less than two hours away. Singapore was out. New York City was in.

Being in the creativity business, we knew we'd have to walk the talk. And so we decided to practice one of our own techniques and look at our challenge through the eyes of someone else. "How would Santa Claus approach a major cash flow crunch?" we asked ourselves. "What would Santa do?"

The answer was obvious. Santa would take to the road. He'd visit people! He'd give gifts!

The costume rentals cost us $300. I would be Santa. Elizabeth would be Mrs. Claus. Val would be a Rudolf, and Tiffany would be the CEO (Chief Elf Officer). Our plan was simple. We'd drive to Manhattan and pay surprise visits to three of our ex-clients, MTV, Met Life, and Price Waterhouse. Once we got past security, we'd give away presents (including our marketing materials) and get people to promise *not* to open them until Christmas morning.

So there we are, the four of us in full Christmas regalia, standing in the tastefully appointed and very marble lobby of Price Waterhouse. Behind the imposing front desk sat three large security guards, none of them named Prancer.

"I'd like to speak to Donna Chandler," I announce, doing my best to channel my inner Santa.

The security guard is not yet in the holiday spirit. His belly does not shake like a bowl full of jelly. "And who shall I say wants to see Ms. Chandler?" he replies with a scowl.

I say nothing, hoping my long white beard will be enough to grant us access. It isn't.

"Don't you recognize me, my friend?" I exclaim. "It's me, Santa Claus!"

"I'll need your real name, sir," the guard replies.

"My *real* name? It's Santa. *Santa Claus.*"

He shakes his head and mumbles something under his breath to the equally large security guard sitting next to him. Scroogily, he pages his way through the company directory and dials the phone.

"Hello," I hear him say. "This is lobby security. There's a guy here to see you. He's dressed liked Santa Claus and won't give me his name."

Other people come and go. Other people are given name badges. Other people walk merrily to the bank of elevators. The four of us just stand there.

And then, the large security guard with no visions of sugarplums dancing in his head calls us forward. "OK, *Santa,*" he grumbles. "You and your little buddies can go up."

The moment we get off the elevator on the 27th floor everyone begins flooding out of their offices. *These aren't auditors at a Big Six accounting firm.* These are big kids in business clothes.

Three women, giggling, lead us to their office. Boldly, they sit me down in an executive chair and, one by one, sit on my lap.

"Have you been good little girls?" I begin.

"Oh *yes*, Santa!"

121

"And what do you want for Christmas?" I ask.

"Better cash flow. A promotion. And a cappuccino machine."

I reach into my bag and pull out a beautifully wrapped gift for each of them.

"Will you promise Santa not to open your presents until Christmas morning?" I ask.

"Oh yes, Santa!"

And then, with a shake of some strategically placed jingle bells, we are off. *On Dasher! On Rudolf! On Cash Flow!*

Out of the office, turning right at the fire drill sign, down 27 floors to the tastefully appointed lobby, past the security guards, and out the door to our next former client, all the way spreading Christmas cheer and marketing materials – ho ho hoping that our former clients will call us the day after the holidays, visions of first quarter results dancing in their hands.

Guess what? They did.

So What?

Ask most business people on a Monday morning to complete the phrase, "Tis the season to be _____," and they are as likely to say "productive" "efficient," or "customer-centric" as they are to say "jolly."

"Jolly" is not a word on the lips of most business people. Neither is "fun," "playful," or "light-hearted." *Seriousness* is the name of the game. *Keeping one's nose to the grindstone. Being professional.* Humor? Something for the weekends. Or Dilbert. And yet, humor, done well, is one of an organization's most valuable human resources. Not only is it free, it dissolves silos, builds rapport, increases morale, and opens the mind to creativity. It's why Isaac Asimov said, "The most exciting phrase to hear in science, the one that heralds new discoveries, is not 'Eureka!' but 'That's funny.'"

My Santa Claus moment at Price Waterhouse is but one example of how this phenomenon works. Not only did my guerilla marketing move get us past security, it got us past the logical, linear, left-brained defenses of the bean-counting auditors on the 27th floor. Sure, we could have opted to set up a business meeting though normal channels, but how much more effective it was to have the client *sitting on my lap* than at the end of a long conference table.

Real estate may be all about *location, location, location*, but breakthrough is all about *dislocation, dislocation, dislocation* – the sudden appearance of the unexpected that reframes perceptions in a way that opens the mind to insight.

"Give me a fulcrum," said Plato two thousand years ago, "and I can move the world."

I say: *Give me humor.*

Now What?

Think of a result you've been trying to get with no success. In what ways might a lighter touch make a difference? How can you use humor to open some locked doors this week?

THE JOE BELINSKY FACTOR

"Time is relative," explained Albert Einstein. "When you touch a hot stove for a second, it feels like eternity. When you sit with a pretty woman for an hour, it feels like a second."

In modern day business, time is not only relative, it's also hard to find. No one has any. Like America's vanishing manufacturing sector, it seems to have gone overseas. Speed is now the name of the game – speed to market, cutting cycle time, and otherwise looking for a thousand caffeinated ways to get things done faster.

Whereas some early inhabitants of North America, the Hopi Indians, assessed the value of their actions by the impact they'd have seven generations into the future, the rest of us are watching the atomic clock. We live in the realm of next quarter, next week, or, *this just in*, next nanosecond.

As a provider of innovation services for the chronographically challenged, I found myself caught up in this phenomenon early in my career – much like a good friend of mine who confessed to me that no matter how early he woke up he always felt late.

Then I met Joe Belinsky.

Joe, a wonderfully bald Professional Development Manager from Goodyear Tire and Rubber, had attended a creative thinking training I conducted and was so pumped by his experience that he sought me out afterwards to wax poetic about the value he received.

"I want to bring you guys into Goodyear," he exclaimed." We really need to get out of the box."

"An excellent idea, Joe," I replied, visions of cash flow dancing in my head. "How would you like to proceed?"

"I'll call when things clarify," he replied.

And he did – one year later.

"Joe Belinsky on Line 2," Nancy tells me, "the guy from Goodyear."

"Cool," I think to myself. "Finally! A prospect who *already* knows the value we provide."

Joe, as I remembered him, is delightful, buoyant, buzzed, and Midwesternly beatific. After the predicable niceties, he explains, "the time isn't quite right – there are *changes* going on and the powers-that-be aren't ready to pull the trigger."

"No problem," I tell Joe. "Call us when the dust settles."

Another year passes.

"Joe Belinsky on Line Two," Nancy exclaims. "The guy from Goodyear."

"Perfect timing!" I think to myself. "We've just lost our biggest account. Maybe, Goodyear can fill the gap."

Joe, once again, is the perfect gentleman, catching me up on everything he cares about – his wife, his kids, the Cleveland Cavaliers, and how he is still using the techniques I had taught him two years before. But... um... you see... there had just been this *reorg* in his department and... well... the time isn't quite right.

"Completely understandable," I tell Joe, doing a quick calculation of all the money we would not be invoicing.

Another year passes. Then another. And another. Then two more after that. Seven years altogether, a Biblical cycle of sorts. Not locusts. Not frogs. Not Egyptians chasing Hebrews. Just seven years of Joe Belinsky calling on Line Two and explaining why it still wasn't the right time for Goodyear to bring us in.

After the third year of this now fairly predictable phenomenon, Joe had become something of a celebrity in our office. If somebody was on "Line Two" it had to be Joe Belinsky. If something was taking longer than expected, it had to do with tires.

Having studied Indian cosmology in my early twenties, it was dawning on me that Joe may have been the harbinger of some kind of esoteric teaching about time. Time, you see, in India, is not measured in the same way it's measured in the West. Indeed, there is a unit of time in India, the Yuga, that once understood, can completely change one's perspective. A Yuga represents a complete epoch or era, spanning somewhere between 12,000 and 24,000 years – or, as the cosmically inclined Indian sages liked to say, a Yuga is "a single in-breath of God." That's a lot of nanoseconds.

It was now seven years from the first time I met Joe Belinsky, seven years from the first time he declared his interest in "bringing us in"– seven years from the first time, Nancy told me he was on Line Two.

The phone rings. It's Joe. Goodyear's yearly trip around our entrepreneurial sun.

"Hey Mitch, guess what?" he blurts.

"Um... let me see. Goodyear has just been bought by Microsoft... headquarters burned down... the CEO was abducted by aliens."

"Nope. It's time."

"It's what?"

"It's time," Joe replies. "It's time to bring you guys in."

And it was. After the requisite due diligence, the contract was signed and we were off to the races, Joe leading the charge and eventually becoming a certified facilitator of a whole bunch of our stuff. Plus, I got to go bowling with Joe and the boys, not to mention watching "The Mummy" on his 57" flat screen TV after a home-cooked meal made by his delightful wife, Joan. For the next two years, 40% of my company's revenues came from Goodyear. And I learned more about tire treads than any seven generations of Hopi elders could ever hope to learn in a Yuga.

SO WHAT?

There is a classic story in the Zen tradition about a monk who lived in a monastery for 20 years doing his best to achieve enlightenment. But no matter what he did, or didn't do, his much sought after enlightenment experience never came.

Disillusioned, he left the monastery and got a job as a sweeper at a local cemetery. One week into it, as he went about his mundane business, a brick he swept off the path hit a tree and broke in half. When it did, he also broke in half. Metaphorically, that is. Something opened in him – something beyond time. The enlightenment came. Not like a customer showing up for an appointment, but like a thief in the night. Not in a monastery surrounded by monks and begging bowls, but in a cemetery, surrounded by gravestones and brooms.

The result the monk sought was *not* a function of time. Indeed, looking back, he realized his mechanistic interpretation of time had been at least partially responsible for his long delayed breakthrough. And while one could easily conclude that his 20 years of monastic life had created the ripe conditions for his spontaneous awakening in the graveyard, the fact remains, he was never – for the entire 20 years of his monkhood – more than a second away from what he was seeking.

He may have never put his hand on a stove for a second or sat with a pretty girl for an hour, but he definitely had his own experience of time's relativity and, even more so, the quickening of what exists beyond time.

I continue to be astounded, daily, by how inaccurate my assessment of time is. I make plans for the day, week, month, and year and rarely does it turn out remotely close to how things actually unfold. Things take longer. Murphy's law abounds.

One thing is clear to me. I don't manage time. Time manages me. And that's not because I'm a bad manager – but because there are some things that cannot be managed in the way we think they need to be managed. Time is one of them. Death is the other. The third? Trying to get your teenage daughter to clean up her room.

"I sat down, one summer, to write my book," confessed Arnold Toynbee, author of *The History of Western Civilization* and 27 years later it was done."

Yes, we need to plan. And yes, strategizing is not a bad thing. But in the end, there is something else going on – a different rhythm, a longer arc, the introduction of timeless truths into our time-warped world – or what I like to call the *Joe Belinsky Factor*.

NOW WHAT?

What project of yours is taking more time than you'd like it to take? If there's something you can do to quicken the process, go for it. But if, in your bones, you know it's simply a function of the Joe Belinsky factor, step back, pause, and breathe deep. It will happen, just not according to your timeline.

A RADICAL NEW WAY TO CAPTURE ATTENTION

There are two kinds of people in the world: those who believetherearetwokindsofpeopleintheworldandthose who don't.

If you find yourself disagreeing with the above statement, congratulations – because it is not necessarily true. I could just have easily said there are *three kinds of people in the world* – those who believe there are three kinds of people, those who don't, and those who don't care.

Or maybe there are *four* kinds of people in the world. Or 397.

Here's my point: The percentage of people who will agree or disagree with my opening statement varies from industry to industry, company to company, and country to country. I cannot tell you how the percentages break out, what the standard deviations are, or what age groups will object most intensely to my assertions. But one thing I *can* tell you is this: the *mindset* of the people who find fault with the opening paragraph tends to be predominantly *left-brained* – the analytical, logical, naysaying point of view.

This is the mindset that describes 90% of my clients – especially those who were attending my "Innovation and Business Growth" class, at GE, one lovely spring day before America's economy melted down – highly intelligent, multi-tracking, no-nonsense "A" players, all of whom would be listening tomorrow to the iconic Jack Welsh standing on the same stage where I was standing today.

My task? To move GE's leaders of the future from their left brain to their right – to help them understand, from the inside out, what Einstein meant when he said "Not everything that counts can be counted, and not everything that can be counted counts."

Having done this work for the past 18 years, I had developed my own Swiss Army knife's worth of *mindset shifting tools* to get the job done – tools that included creative thinking techniques, experiential challenges, storytelling, humor, the right use of music, movement, juggling, and emergent design.

Two hours into the session, things were going just fine. GE's best and brightest had given up their fear I would make them sing Kumbaya, and I had given up my fear that someone would discover my graduate school education was in *poetry*, not business.

At 10:00 a.m. my advanced facilitator skills kick in, and I notice my bladder is full – the kind of full that, If I didn't respond soon, would result in my hopping from one foot to the other.

Priorities newly clarified, I teach the group a creative thinking technique that will keep them busy for enough time for me to relieve myself.

Technique taught, I make my way up the aisle, find the bathroom, and do what 95% of men do when they pee – aim dead center for the round hockey puck-shaped thingee in the middle of the urinal.

The bathroom, also one of GE's best and brightest, is about the size of a New York City studio apartment, complete with a shiny marble counters and a week's worth of carefully folded towels.

Mission accomplished, I flush, check my face in the mirror, and retrace my steps to the high-tech amphitheater. Upon entering, everyone turns around to look at me. Half of them are laughing. The other half are smiling. And if there was *another* half lurking somewhere beyond the laws of earthly mathematics, they would have been madly texting the details of what they had just found so amusing.

I am tickled that GE's best and brightest are happy to see me, but I am also perplexed. This is not the usual welcome I receive upon returning from a bathroom.

Confused, I shoot a glance at Ben, my business partner, in the back of the room. He is wildly gesticulating, Marcel Marceau on steroids.

"Your mic is on," he seems to be saying, pointing at his lapel.

"Hmmm," I think to myself. "My mic is on… my MIC is on. Oops."

From what I can tell, I had just broadcasted my entire bathroom experience to 75 global business leaders of the future. I had to think fast.

"Oh that?" I say, taking another step down the aisle to the podium. "All part of the day's design. Totally intentional. My attempt to…"

The rest of my sentence is drowned out by laughter. They will have none of it. Of course, they won't. What I am saying is ridiculous, but because the *way* I said it was entertaining and self-effacing, they were not only forgiving, but also suddenly much lighter and more engaged than before I'd left the room.

It would not be an exaggeration to say that in the three years of facilitating innovation sessions at GE, I had never seen a group of people as engaged as this particular group. In some strange way, in five minutes I had accomplished what usually took me at least an hour – bringing a room full of left-brained, bottom-line-oriented business people to a fully present state of mind, open to whatever was going to happen next.

So What?

Who knew that I would learn something extraordinary about the art of opening corporate minds by peeing in a GE urinal? If you had asked me earlier that day what my biggest breakthrough would be, I doubt the word "bathroom" would have entered the conversation. But that's where the breakthrough came from – an unplanned, spontaneous moment beyond my ability to conceive.

The literature on innovation overflows with stories about moments like this – "happy accidents" – unanticipated occurrences that triggers extraordinary results.

The discovery of Penicillin? An accident in the lab. The Post-it note? Unplanned – the list go on an on: vulcanized rubber, LSD, Viagra, and Velcro˚, just to name a few.

These breakthroughs were not so much *invented* as they were *stumbled upon*. Recent research supports this phenomenon – 75% of all product breakthroughs are *unplanned.*

My bathroom moment at GE was consistent with this research. Although I had designed my agenda to include five different "mind shift" catalysts, it was the *unplanned* moment in the bathroom that had the biggest impact. In a nanosecond, my amplified peeing got people out of their heads, jumpstarted spontaneity, established presence, sparked laughter, elevated mood, increased focus, created a unified field of attention, and perhaps most importantly, dissolved the boundary between the "all knowing expert" and the "unknowing student".

All of us, no matter what our profession, need to stay open to the unexpected and mine its value. Instead of prematurely judging it as bad or wrong, we need to get curious and explore its possibilities. Like Alexander Fleming did with penicillin. Like Art Fry did with the Post-it note. Like Charles Goodyear did with vulcanized rubber.

Will there be mistakes with no redeeming value? Yes, there will. But there will be just as many blunders that will spark new insights, new products, and new ways of doing business. That is, if we are willing to give up playing victim and begin playing jazz.

Now What?

Think of a recent mistake you have made on the job – something you wished had turned out differently. Take a few minutes now to bring your mistake to mind. Put aside any feelings of embarrassment or shame that accompanied this unplanned moment. What can you learn from it? And, if you had it to do all over again, what might you have done differently to "save the day."

A Man of Few Words

Last year I wrote a 360-page book that attracted the attention of one of the world's most celebrated literary agents. He was so moved by my writing that he immediately took me on as a client and, one week later, sold my book to one of New York's leading publishing houses. My editor there absolutely loved the book, but felt that I had "gone on too long" in several places and requested that I tighten up the writing before publication, which, I am pleased to say, I did without much complaint, leaving me with a much leaner and meaner 272-page manuscript.

The publisher's *focus group*, however, a vital part of the editorial process, noted that one of the chapters – the longest one – seemed better suited for the sequel – an observation, I thought, that was actually quite astute and also inspiring, as I had not, until that time, thought my book was good enough to merit a sequel. So I got to work, excised the too-long chapter, tweaked a few segues here and there, and, in just a matter of days, was the proud papa of a still-very-commanding 189-page tome, "destined," my publisher declared, for *The New York Times* Best Seller list.

My publicist, an industry heavyweight since 1973 and an upstanding member of the American Academy of Arts and Sciences, was delighted to be representing me, but suggested, with all due respect, that I should more carefully consider my demographic – a slice of the global population, her research indicated, that was increasingly struggling with ADD and, if I was still committed to my book becoming a commercial success, I needed to seriously consider trimming it down to 120 pages, which she explained, was the ideal length for my particular market.

While I found it a bit disconcerting to re-enter the editorial process once again, what my publicist had said made perfect sense and, since one of the reasons I had written the book in the first place was to make the extra money I needed to pay for my daughter's college education, I battened down whatever hatches I had left and got busy. It took me three weeks to make the changes, but with the unflagging encouragement of my best friend and some top-shelf tequila, I nailed it, leaving me with 120 pages of what my editor was now referring to as my "modern day Rilkean prose".

Not only had I gotten my book down to fighting weight, I finally understood what Michelangelo meant when he explained, centuries ago, his process for sculpting his iconic David. "I simply took away everything that wasn't." Though outwardly my book was now smaller than before, *inwardly*, I had been transported back to the Renaissance and the emerging essence of my opus grande. Life was good.

When I showed the manuscript to my wife, a highly intuitive visionary with a knack for seeing what was invisible to me, she was miffed. One hundred and twenty pages, my dear wife explained, was more like a "booklet" than a book and did I really want to be known as a writer of booklets?

She was right, of course. What writer wants to be associated with the word "booklet?" Certainly not me. So I dropped my 120-page paradigm and decided to cut my manuscript in half until I had the perfect 60-page story that could easily be serialized for *Esquire* – one 15-page story per month for four consecutive months, the first one appearing in September, the same month my daughter would be heading off to college.

The idea to have my writing serialized in *Esquire* was an unexpected stroke of genius, I must say, since many a serialized story in that highly regarded publication, I came to realize, had caught the attention of Hollywood's biggest studios, many of whom paid big bucks to buy the movie rights. By the way, I would be getting not only a screen credit and a hefty paycheck, but would be invited to the Oscars if the movie made it big.

What I *didn't* see coming was the angst of my editor's mistress, a stunning, red-headed, erudite woman who, though she adored my writing, believed strongly that Chapter Two was far superior to my other three chapters. Since she was angry at her editor/boyfriend for spending Valentine's Day with his wife and kids, the said mistress threatened not to have sex with him for six months unless he agreed to *only* publish my Chapter Two. This was, shall we say, somewhat deflating for me, but I had to agree that of the four chapters, Chapter Two was, by far, the strongest.

As I reflected on this unexpected turn of events while walking the three blocks back to my hotel, it dawned on me that buried *within* the 15-page chapter that my editor's mistress preferred, abided the perfect poem – *an epic poem* – a classic genre of writing, I believed, that could easily be revived for the modern-day reader, a genre that would deeply honor my early roots as a poet. Wow! How great would it be to have my epic poem published in Esquire and reach an audience of millions!

My editor loved the idea, but when he pitched it to his protégé, a 22-year-old wunderkind from Hong Kong recently hired to help *Esquire* tap into the Far East millennial market, he discovered that while Asian millennials DO read poetry, they do not read epic poetry. Haiku is their preferred medium, it being so ultimately *pristine* and, in today's Twitter-dominated marketplace, the perfect length to deliver a powerful message to as many people as possible in the shortest amount of time.

Was I reluctant to translate my epic poem into haiku form? Yes I was, although, upon further reflection, there was something about the challenge that intrigued me, having always been a big fan of the form and, in fact, when I was 22 myself, owned a first edition of Basho's haikus, a beautifully crafted tome complete with tissue paper overlays of the most elegant calligraphy I had ever seen. So, haiku it was – a form, I soon came to realize, that was easy to imitate, but hard to master – kind of like the difference, as Mark Twain once wrote, between lightning and a lightning bug. So I drank a lot of sake, downloaded some Koto music, and got to work.

In less than a week, I had myself a stellar haiku, one that my editor, his mistress, and protégé were so taken with that they took me out to dinner that night to *the* most expensive sushi restaurant in all of Manhattan. *Finally*, after months of endless editing I had the perfect piece of writing for publication! Hallelujah!

What I didn't understand at that precise moment was that the sales staff of *Esquire's* advertising department, newly back from an intensive Tony Robbins seminar on the Left Coast, was so unbelievably empowered that they had just broken all previous sales records and sold out every single inch of space in the magazine for the next four months. Translation? There was no room left in the magazine for my haiku. All contracts had been signed and unless *Esquire* wanted to pay their advertisers hefty rebate fees, my haiku wouldn't be appearing for at least five months, which meant, of course, that I would not see a paycheck until February, 2016, which was several months after the due date for my daughter's freshman year tuition.

Though I admit to being understandably devastated at that moment in time, my spirits soon lifted upon hearing the latest news from my editor. The September issue, he explained, would feature a two-page spread by one of the world's most up-and-coming graphic designers – a creative genius from Amsterdam with well over five million Twitter followers. If I could reduce my haiku to a *single word*, the designer would find a way to feature my word in his spread – the centerpiece of the September issue,

I was told – an issue that would be greatly promoted by the sales staff and, as a result, would likely bring a global tidal wave of attention to my word.

Friday is my deadline, but... um... uh... I'm having some trouble with the final phase of the editing process. I wouldn't say I'm "stuck," just needing a bit of input. What do *you* think the word should be? Please understand that I'm not asking you to *write* the piece for me, just suggest some possibilities and I, in conjunction with my wife, editor, editor's mistress, protégé, publicist, and advertising team, will select one.

If I end up using the word that you suggest, be assured, I will generously acknowledge you in my anticipated acceptance speech.

So What?

OK. Maybe I flashed my poetic license just a bit much in the above piece, but so what? And according to whom? Did I go too far? Only if you didn't come along for the ride. If you are a creative, self-directed person who likes to blaze new trails, know that you are going to be confronted, again and again, by the societal machine of "good taste," commercialism, and political correctness. There is no way around it. Everyone is going to have an opinion. Everyone will have a unique point of view. That's not up for debate. What *is* up for debate is *how you respond*. Will you be humble enough to consider the fact that others' input has the potential to help you take your creations to the next level of cool? Or will you sell yourself out to the highest (for)bidder and concede to the collective hallucination of the "powers-that-be?"

Now What?

Think of one of your projects that you are passionate about. What kind of feedback are you receiving? Is there a pattern to this feedback? If so, does it make sense to you? In what ways might you be willing to tweak your approach? In what ways may you have prematurely conceded to this feedback, giving up the core of your own calling for no other reason than to appease your objectors?

ISLAND OF THE FIREFLIES

The year was 1981. Ronald Reagan was the U. S. President. Lady Diana had just married Prince Charles. And I had just landed a job in Los Angeles with the highly respected consulting firm, The Inner Game Corporation, which was newly immersed in the process of landing a big contract with Atari, the $900 million dollar maker of the Pacman video game.

Atari was enamored with Inner Game's learning methods and Inner Game was enamored with actually making enough money to have the time to play Pacman. As negotiations heated up, my new company's chief negotiator decided to sweeten the deal by promising we would deliver, in time for Atari's computer summer camp, an interactive, make-your-own-adventure children's book that would teach kids how to learn faster, smarter, and with way less stress than ever before.

I was thrilled to hear that Inner Game's team had closed the deal. That is, until I heard *who* was going to write the book – *me* – and when the deadline was – *30 days from the day I was offered the assignment.*

First of all, I had never written a book. Second of all, I was still trying to figure out what the Inner Game business was all about. And third of all, see #1. Thirty days did not seem like a lot of time to write a book, so I decided to seek the counsel of the only professional writer I knew, the co-author of *Tron*.

"Six months," she told me. "This is a six month project. Don't even think about writing a book in a one month. That would be insane."

But that's not what I wanted to hear. What I wanted to hear was "Hey, Mitch, anything's possible. If you get your ducks in a row, you can do this!"

So I thanked Bonnie for her input, returned to the office, and accepted the assignment.

The first thing I knew I needed to do was change my living situation. Sharing a house with ten people was unlikely to yield the kind of concentration I would need to write my book, so I moved out and rented a cabin a few miles away.

The next thing I knew I needed to do was come up the plot and a setting for the story, so I hustled over to the nearest bookstore and bought an illustrated book about dwarves living underground. *Why* these dwarves were living underground, I hadn't the foggiest clue, but there was something about the pictures and the idea of society's outsiders creating their own, invisible world that really got to me. Upon returning to my cabin, I ripped the pages out of the book and taped them to my walls.

Knowing time was short, I unplugged from everything I could think of – shaving, changing my clothes, sunlight, friends, exercise, balanced meals, asking people how they were doing, going for walks, and a whole lot of other things I didn't have time to plan unplugging from. I just sat in my cabin for 30 days and did my thing, which was a bouillabaisse of writing, thinking about writing, rewriting, editing, staring at walls, daydreaming, thinking about dwarves, making lists, drinking coffee, feeling desperate, and wondering how I got into this predicament in the first place. For seven of those 30 days, I did not sleep a wink.

If my task had been to write a normal story, with a beginning, middle and end, that would have been one thing, but that was not my task. My task was to write a make-your-own-adventure story – a story with multiple endings – 28 to be more precise – *and* a deck of cards to accompany the book *and* a floppy disk with clues that would help the kids make wise choices about which path to follow in the book.

I lived in my pajamas. I sat at my desk. I did not floss. I did not cultivate friendships, date, do any volunteer work, read the Sports section, wonder if I should have gone into my father's business, read Rumi, or try to save the world. Surrounded by dwarves and more than few doubts, I found myself drifting further and further out to sea. The undertow? My ridiculous deadline and a morbid fascination for attempting the impossible.

Though I was living alone, I was far from lonely. A houseful of women lived just a stone's throw from my door – women who would show up daily with a tray of food and flowers. Other people would also show up, friends who were concerned about my state of mind. They wanted me to "get out" or "exercise" or "see a movie." I knew they meant well, but, from my perspective, their suggestions were a royal waste of time. Get out? Exercise? Go to the 12-plex? Are you kidding me? I was a man on a mission, interested in only one thing – writing my book in 30 days – which, I am happy to announce, I was well on my way to doing when, 20 days into it, I hit a wall. Not just *any* wall. THE wall – the wall from whence the phrase "hitting a wall" originated. Not a prosaic brick wall. Not a sturdy looking cinder block wall. Not a nicely photographed wall covered with ivy. No. I'm talking about the primal wall – the one with the kind of Olympic dimension that keeps everyone out.

That kind of wall.

Staying up late didn't help. Getting up early didn't help. Nor did getting up late or staying up early. Nothing helped. But I needed help, and knew I needed to leave my abode to get that help. It wasn't a mystery *where* this help abided. I knew *exactly* where it was – at a computer school in Silicon Valley, a school for gifted young geeks – one of Atari's "charter schools" that I, as an Inner Game consultant, had access to should my research require it, which it did.

The first thing I did when I got to the school was ask the teacher who his most creative student was. "Him!" the teacher announced in a heartbeat, pointing to a curly-headed kid in the back of the room. "That's Lewis. He's the only one you need to talk to."

So I made my way over to the lad, introduced what was left of my self, and asked if he'd listen to my story and share *his* ideas for where he thought it should go. When I got to the part about where I was stuck, he laughed, paused for a few seconds, then launched into major tribal storytelling mode, me feverishly taking notes. The amulet? A brilliant touch. The evil Dr. Stuckenmeyer? Fantastic. The quicksand river theme? Pure genius.

Thanking Lewis profusely, I made my way over to Atari's Headquarters where I was ushered into the office of a man who not only made a lot more money than I did, but had apparently slept the night before. After the predicable niceties, he asked how the book was coming. I told him the whole story – the first half, which I had dreamed up in my dwarf-infused cabin for 20 days and the *second* half, which Lewis, the boy wonder, had channeled to me just 30 minutes ago.

The VP sat there, riveted. "Wow," he said. "I can't wait to read it."

The next ten days were a blur. Me in my cabin. Me in my pajamas. Me sitting at the same desk, knocks on the same door by worried friends, perfectly timed visits from *other* friends bearing tofu salad sandwiches and asking if I wanted a massage. They came and they went, two sides of the same coin, but I was living in a realm where the currency had nothing to do with two sides of anything – not good or bad, not up or down, not in or out. The world I was inhabiting was a world where thought and action had merged, where words made flesh, and flesh fell away, where night and day didn't matter and matter held no sway. Yes, the clock was ticking but so was the unspeakable glory of letting the finished story, after 28 days, shake through me onto the paper like some kind of divine palsy.

Done! I was done! Now the only thing left to do was to drive the 200 books, just printed the night before, down to computer camp in San Diego.

I arrived at the exact same moment Atari's VP of Education arrived, both of us pulling into the same parking lot. She got out of her car, trailed by her entourage. I got out of mine, trailed by no one, book in hand, moving towards her in slow motion *Chariot's of Fire* mode, placing the book, like a baton, in her outstretched hand.

"We got it!" she announced, holding the book high over her head. *"We got it!"*

So What?

None of us know what we're capable of. We may think we know, but we don't. And most of the people we know don't know what we're capable of either because they don't know what *they're* capable of. While there is nothing wrong with not knowing what we're capable of, there *is* something wrong with not being willing to find out. And often that willingness requires a letting go of what we know and *how* we know we know and *what* we do and *when*, an untethering of the too small boat we've been playing with in the bathtub of our lives. Your friends may think you've lost it. Your loved ones may try to reel you in. Your sirens may howl, but that's just how it goes. For now, here's all you need to remember: Let go of fear. Persist and ask for help when you need it. None of us are here alone, even if it feels like that a lot of the time. There are angels everywhere – angels and muses and guides and clues. All you need to do is say YES and trust your creative process.

NOW WHAT?

Think of a challenge before you that feels impossible. Maybe it's a move you want to make, a career you want to change, a project you want to launch, a product you want to invent, a school you want to start, or a wrong you want to right. Whatever it is, bring it to mind. Now close your eyes and feel it. Imagine it's some time down the road and your venture has succeeded. What do you see? What do you feel? And what can you do, this week, to begin creating the conditions you need to bring this vital venture of yours to life?

A Corkboard Grows in Brooklyn

Some entrepreneurs, when starting their business, watch the bottom line. Some watch the Dow Jones. My business partner and I watched a corkboard. Not just any corkboard, mind you – a 3 foot square by 3 foot square corkboard in Brooklyn attached to a wall in the only room of my apartment that qualified as an office –a prison cell of a space with a desk, file cabinet, and phone – a realm we affectionately referred to as the "International Headquarters of Idea Champions," a start up with assets rivaling only a junior high school lemonade stand.

Armed with little more than what remained of a $15,000 loan, some business cards, and a 1984 Pontiac Sunbird we never had to lock because our local car thieves felt sorry for us, our corkboard soon became the epicenter of our universe. Not because it was awe inspiring, but because of the index cards pinned to it, each inscribed with the names of a company we planned to talk to in the coming month.

We would lean back in our chairs, gaze at the corkboard, and feel good about ourselves. Having no clients, technically speaking, we weren't "successful," but we felt successful. The names on those index cards were *placeholders of possibility,* proof we were making progress, progress that by any stretch of the imagination was little more than a stretch of the imagination – but the *kind of stretch* that kept our vision alive and on fire – the kind of fire that would, just a few years later, be fanned into the flames of a multi-million-dollar enterprise.

So What?

The word "success" comes from the Latin word "sucedere" meaning "to take one step after the other." Isn't that what success is all about – *progressing* – successively taking steps toward your goal? For most of us, however, "success" means something else – something huge like winning the Nobel Peace Prize or being elected President.

A few weeks ago, while walking with a friend, I saw a penny on the ground. I bent down, picked it up, and mumbled something about it being "only a penny." But my friend had a different story to tell. For him, that penny was an indication of riches to come, a sign from Lakshmi, the Goddess of Wealth, that I was walking the right path. All I needed to do, he explained, was be grateful for my good fortune. The story he told in just a few sentences completely changed my relationship to money.

He saw it one way. I saw it another. But the way he saw it totally recalibrated the way I now think about success.

Now What?

Bring to mind a current project of yours – a project for which results are showing up more slowly than you'd imagined. Now take a few minutes to jot down all of the progress you've made so far, including all of the little stuff. Then read the list aloud. How does it make you feel?

THE PAW PHONE

During the past 25 years I have facilitated more than 1,000 creative thinking sessions for a wide variety of heavy hitting organizations – everyone from MTV to GE to government think tanks. I've worked with left-brained people, right-brained people, and reptilian-brained people. Along the way, I've developed quite a few strategies to get people out of their heads and into a more robust realm of possibility. But the biggest breakthroughs I've seen have had less to do with my methods than they did with *spontaneous occurrences*. Like the time a porcelain hotel dog became the catalyst for a game-changing product idea.

I was leading a daylong ideation session for a large telecommunications company when it was time for lunch. Everyone left the room, visions of turkey wraps in their heads, when I noticed a peculiar looking porcelain dog next to a plastic fern in the corner of the room – the kind of kitschy piece of Americana you'd pass at a yard sale, mumbling to yourself that this was absolutely the last time you'd ever go to a yard sale.

Somehow, I found myself drawn to the porcelain dog and, being in a particularly playful mood, picked it up and placed it on a folding chair in the middle of the room. Tickled by its absolute uselessness and lack of beauty, I put my hat on its weird, little head and went about my business of getting ready for the afternoon session. Five minutes later, the head of HR walks in, takes off his power tie, and places it around the dog's neck. Then an IT guy enters, removes his "Hello My Name Is" badge and sticks it on the dog's chest. A well-dressed woman then removes her necklace and wraps it around the dog's waist.

There in the middle of the room, unleashed, unbarking, but no longer unloved, sits the perfect brainstorm session mascot – a 3D embodiment of our collective mind.

The rest of the participants return soon enough and gather around the porcelain dog as if it was the Holy Grail. Someone tapes a cell phone to its back, a woman wraps a scarf around his neck, and another person puts tape over its mouth.

Something is happening that has nothing to do with my design for the day. A curious kind of creativity portal is manifesting before my eyes.

"OK!" I blurt, as people return from lunch. "What cool, new product ideas come to mind when you look at good ole' Fido here?"

Ideas flood the room.

In a few minutes, it is clear that a big idea is emerging – the idea for a niche product for a market no one in this room had considered before – *animals* – especially *dogs* who lived with blind or disabled people – animals who could easily be trained to push a large red button on a one-button phone any time their masters were unable to. What soon became known, in that room, as the *Paw Phone*.

"Pet idea" conceived, we spent the next ten minutes fleshing it out, adding it to the list of the other big ideas to be presented at the end of the day to an independent focus group, who would be joining us. The funny thing? Of the ten ideas we pitched to the focus group that day, the Paw Phone was rated the third highest. Woof woof.

So What?

Good ideas can come from anyone at any time and in any place. While it is impossible to predict precisely when and where the good ideas will manifest, it *is* possible to predict the optimal conditions that will make it more likely for good ideas to appear.

The spirit of playfulness, one of these conditions, manifested itself gloriously in the Paw Phone session. I simply followed my hunch that the porcelain dog was part of the creative process. I didn't know *how*. I couldn't know. I could only trust my instincts and my past experience that often seemingly random catalysts are the DNA for breakthroughs. That and the fact that when we enter the state of *not trying* we often get the best results.

Carl Jung understood this phenomenon: "The creation of something new," he said, "is not accomplished by the intellect, but by the play instinct arising from inner necessity. The creative mind plays with the object it loves."

And yet, in the corporate world, playfulness is often demonized, marginalized, and ignored – as if it was a symptom of the worst kind of anti-business, slacker mentality.

It's time to shed the notion that work always has to be so serious – that grunting and groaning is the preferred response and that laughter means you're not working. Baloney. Untrue. Insane. *This just in: Life is supposed to be fun.* And since work is a part of life, it too needs to be fun – especially when you find yourself in the middle of a brainstorming session trying to discover a better way to do this, that, or the other thing.

NOW WHAT?

On a scale of 1-10, with 10 being the highest possible rating, how serious is your workplace? How serious are the meetings you attend? And if it's 7 or more, what can you do to lighten things up?

Dreaming the Solution

Elias Howe, the inventor of the lock-stitch sewing machine, was stumped. For years he had been working diligently on his new invention, but for the life of him, he could not come up with the right design for the needle. With the eyelet of the needle positioned near the middle of the shaft, the needle kept breaking – something that made no sense to him. Then one night, exhausted and confused, he had a dream. In the dream, a menacing group of natives surrounded him, each holding a large spear and directing him to the "place of execution" – a large caldron of boiling water. Just as he was about to be lowered into the cauldron, Elias looked up and noticed that at the top of each spear was a small hole, the perfect design, he realized, for the needle. Jumping out of bed, he carved a prototype of what he had just seen. And the rest, as they say, is history.

A few years after I read this story, I had a similar experience. It was the night before I was going to be leading a two-day brainstorming session for a high-tech packaging company and even though I had already designed the meeting, I still felt something was missing.

In my dream, I saw a 6 x 6 grid, each square filled with a different word or phrase. The purpose of the grid was to help people make new connections between previously unrelated elements of the problem they were trying to solve.

When I woke up, I wrote it all down, showered, and drove the 150 miles to the meeting site. As I drove, one question consumed me: Do I teach the technique I had dreamed the night before or do I go with what I had already planned?

In honor of Elias Howe, I decided to teach the new technique.

The people in my session, mostly engineers and chemists, loved it. Not only did the technique make sense to them, it triggered some extraordinary ideas. So extraordinary, in fact, that when it was time for them to rate each technique at the end of the session, the one I dreamed the night before (now known as the "Idea Lottery technique") received the highest rating.

So What?

The subconscious mind is an incredible resource that far too many of us neglect, deny, or undervalue. After our conscious mind exhausts itself with trying to generate solutions, the challenge passes to the subconscious mind, our own private think tank, that works overtime to originate breakthrough ideas. Einstein, for example, conducted what he called "thought experiments" – a fancy name for daydreaming – when he was stuck for a solution. Salvador Dali and Thomas Edison took naps during their workday, knowing that when they awoke, they would have greater access to the part of their brain where non-obvious solutions abided. The pre-condition for these breakthrough cognitions is almost always an extended time of frustration and fruitless effort. Yes, the darkest hour comes before the dawn. And it is the subconscious mind, the intuitive dreamer in all of us, that is the bringer of the light.

NOW WHAT?

Bring a challenging problem, challenge, or frustration to mind – a project you've been struggling with. Tonight, after getting into bed, remember it. Mull it over in your mind and tell yourself you will remember your dream in the morning. When you awake, before doing anything else, write your dream down. Then reflect on it. See what message is there for you. If your dream is jumbled, surreal, or nonsensical, tune into a compelling part of your dream – an image, word, or feeling that captures your attention. Explore the clues embedded in that part of your dream.

KNEE JERK MEETS NAYSAYING

Most Fortune 500 companies have some kind of corporate strategy in place for ratcheting up their innovation efforts. Consultants are hired. CEOs give pep talks. And internal initiatives are launched. To the casual observer, it looks good, but in the end, few of these initiatives ever amount to much. In fact, research indicates that less than 10% of all corporate "change efforts" are successful.

Why such a low percentage? It depends on whom you ask. Senior leaders see it as a workforce issue. The workforce sees it as a senior leadership issue. And the occasional in-house astrologer sees it as a Gemini in Pluto issue. In other words, no one really knows.

Here's how I see it: The main reason why most corporate innovation initiatives fall short can be traced to the Cro-Magnon way most people give and receive feedback – especially when it comes to ideas that threaten the status quo.

Case in point.

Some years ago, Lucent Technologies asked me to facilitate a daylong "products of the future" session for 75 of their best and brightest. The pay was good. The work was interesting. And I was going to have carte blanche to design the day the way I wanted. *Or so I thought.*

The woman who contacted me reported to the CEO. So far so good. Her concept of the session was spot on – that the CEO and his direct reports (a new rock band?) – would make an appearance at the end of the day to give their feedback on the best five ideas. Theoretically, this made perfect sense. But theory and reality are two different things. Like the difference between asking your teenage daughter to clean up her room and her actually doing it. Senior leaders, in my experience, are not very skillful when it comes to giving feedback – especially in response to big, bold ideas that require massive investment. In reality, the word "feedback," to most senior leaders, is code for "Let me tell you why your idea sucks."

As a facilitator of the creative process, I could not in good faith set participants up for a fall. So I declared my need to meet with the CEO at least a one week before the session to teach him a technique that would enable him and his team to give effective, *humane* feedback.

"Impossible," came the response. "Our CEO is a very busy man, and besides, he doesn't like consultants."

"OK," I said, going all in, "then I respectfully decline your offer to facilitate the session."

"I don't understand where you're going with this," she responded.

"If you want results," I explained, "we've got to find a way to ensure that the feedback at the end of the day is effective. I am not going to walk the 75 participants into an ambush."

"OK," she conceded. "But the best I can do is get you five minutes with him, at the coffee break, just before the feedback session begins."

"I'll take it."

Fast forward two months. From 8:30 a.m. – 2:45 p.m., 75 brilliant Lucent technologists dreamed up products that made my head spin. At 2:45, they selected five of their best ideas. At 3:00, it was coffee break time, me waiting for the CEO and his not-so-merry band of direct reports.

I envision him to be a tall man, silver-haired, with a large Rolex and a steely look in his eyes. He is, I am surprised to see, my height, wearing a Mickey Mouse t-shirt, loafers, and no socks. I shake his hand and introduce myself.

"Rich," I begin, "how would you like to learn a technique that will take all the dread out of giving feedback? You'll get what you need and the 75 brainstormers will get what they need to take their ideas to the next level."

He looks at me as if I'd just given him the cure to cancer and said, "You're on."

"Here's how it works," I continue. "When an idea is pitched, first you say what you *like* about the idea – the upside, what's promising. After a few likes, you then express your *concerns* – what you probably wanted to say in the first place – but for each concern you express, it's your responsibility to follow it with a *suggestion*, a way to resolve your concern. Got it?"

"Got it."

"Oh, and one more thing. If you forget to use the technique, do I have your permission to remind you?"

"Absolutely."

The first pitch was excellent – a compelling idea for a futuristic telecommunications platform that was mind blowing. I acknowledge the presenter and give the floor to the CEO – reminding him to use the technique I'd just taught him, which he did for, oh, maybe 30 seconds.

After that? It was *Apocalypse Now* meets *The Godfather* with a little Don Rickles in Vegas thrown in – a scene I'd witnessed countless times before in corporate America – the knee-jerk, reptilian-brained tendency to look for what's *wrong* with an idea before what's *right*.

Speaking into the mic, in my best baritone imitation of the Wizard of Oz, I intervene.

"OH MR. CEO... oh head of a large and profitable telecommunications company. Remember the LCS technique! *First your likes, then your concerns, then your suggestions.*"

Clearly, the man I am correcting is not accustomed to being told what to do, especially by an outside consultant. Sheepishly, he smiles, thanks me for the reminder, and returns to the technique.

The rest of the session goes off without a hitch. Seventy-five empowered Lucent technologists. Seven benevolent senior leaders. Five game changing ideas, newly refined and on their way to becoming products of the future.

So What?

Ideas are often thought of as being a "dime a dozen." That conclusion, however, is less about them being inconsequential, than it is about people not knowing how to elicit their value. Of course, not every idea is worth developing, but far too many good ideas are lost because the person to whom the idea is pitched is blinded by his or her own knee-jerk reactions. The literature is filled with examples: the steam engine, the Macintosh, the television, FedEx, Mrs. Field's Cookies – all were pitched to the "powers-that-be" and all were victims of this kneejerk, naysaying, idea-killing behavior. And though many senior leaders beat the drums for "out of the box thinking," when push comes to shove, their drumming sounds more like fingernails on the edge of an office desk than a conga player with fire in his eyes. Many business leaders think it's their *job* to look for what's wrong.

Now What?

Think about your style of responding to new ideas. Do you listen? Do you give meaningful feedback in a humane way? And what about your company? Do people know how to give and receive feedback? Do they take the time? If not, what can you do this week to begin turning things around, at least within your own sphere of influence?

When Oversleeping Before a Big Presentation Is a Good Thing to Do

Everyone who works for a living has some kind of ritual they've created, consciously or unconsciously, to manage their stress and increase their odds of achieving success, much like basketball players go through the same dribble-the-ball-and-cross-themselves routine every time they step to the foul line. Mozart exercised before he composed. Samuel Johnson needed a purring cat in the room before he wrote. My son, at 4, had to say good night to "Clowney," his paper mache mask on the wall, before going to sleep.

I am very familiar with this phenomenon, especially when I'm on the road.

When I enter my hotel room, I walk to the desk and remove all those completely unnecessary laminated tent cards promoting Happy Hour and the nearest take-out pizza restaurant. I deposit them in a corner of the room, along with the coffee maker I will never use. Email checked, I flop down on the bed and turn on the TV, hoping to find the "Big Game." I think about unpacking, but dismiss the thought, reasoning that the night is still young and I've just flown such a long distance I deserve a little down time. Although I've packed my gym clothes, there is very little chance I am going to work out, now that I am getting hungry and room service is only a phone call away. Grilled salmon is my first choice, though there's always a chance I will go for the chicken, especially if it comes with a side of mashed potatoes. When the waiter knocks, 15 minutes later than promised, and asks me where to put the tray of food, I point to the bed. Meal consumed, mini-bar explored, I watch the news, ESPN highlights, review my agenda for the next day, and proceed to fill out a stack of index cards, summarizing the key elements of my session, titles highlighted in yellow, start times noted in the top right-hand corner of each card. Then I call the front desk and request a wake-up call for 5:30 a.m., set my iPhone alarm, floss, brush my teeth, notice I'm chubbier than I used to be, and go to bed. When I wake up five hours later, I shower, shave, answer the call of nature, and review my note cards. Then, 90 minutes before my presentation, I make my way to the meeting room so I can set it up just the way I like and have enough time left over just in case the hotel has misplaced my supplies.

My routine, no matter how quirky, works every time, providing me with exactly what I need to be "in the zone" when the client introduces me to a roomful of business people wondering if I'm going to ask them to sing Kumbaya. Did I say *every* time? If I did, please forgive me. That would be an exaggeration. You see, I have to *wake up* when the wake-up call comes. And last week, I did not. Actually, the wake-up call never came. No one called me. Nor did my iPhone, set to vibrate, rouse me from my jet-lagged sleep. The result? I woke up five minutes before I was supposed to meet my client in Ballroom "A". *Five minutes.* That's not a lot of time to shower, shave, answer nature's call, meditate, dress, review a stack of note cards, and descend 12 flights to the lobby.

What followed was an outtake from a Marx Brothers movie – Groucho on speed – my own hyper-animated, near-death experience in which I did not see the light, only my crazed face in the bathroom mirror, blood dripping down my neck from shaving too fast.

Only one thing was clear: With this kind of start to the day, my presentation was going to be a huge disappointment – not the outcome I was seeking, this being the first time I'd be speaking to the senior leadership team of one of the world's largest banks.

The elevator door opens. I press "G". The elevator stops at each and every floor. Each. And. Every. Floor. It. Stops. At. Each. And. Every. Floor.

173

We finally get to the lobby. I do not let women and children go first. Glancing at my watch, I notice it is only 7:07 – what political pollsters would call "within the margin of error."

I race-walk across the lobby. Still bleeding, I enter Ballroom "A", doing my best impersonation of a Zen monk. My client smiles, asks if I had a good night's sleep, and mumbles something about PowerPoint. I nod, exchange a few pleasantries, and say nothing of the Fellini movie I'm in. Though I'm relieved I've made it to the room, in the back of my mind, I'm filled with doubt. *Am I ready? Am I prepared? Am I good to go?*

People are filing into the room, checking their email. No one has a clue what I've just been through. No one cares. Two minutes before show time, I realize I have a choice, the same choice I have every day of my life. *I can be present and trust what I know – or I can obsess on everything that seems to be wrong.* I choose the former, as the AV guy mics me up, hands me the remote, and wishes me good luck.

So What?

Unless you've been living in a trailer park your entire life, I'm sure you've met more than a few a well-educated people who thought they needed yet another degree in order to really make it in their field. Like physicists who can prove that a person never actually arrives anywhere because he or she is always only halving the distance to their destination, many of us find ourselves in a state of "never really being there" – a bouillabaisse of doubt, anxiety, and odd, little compensatory behaviors. Peel the onion of most business leaders and you will likely find a smart person scared shitless of being outed as an impostor. And so begins the endless quest for *more* – more information, more data, more knowledge, more degrees, more preparation – and whatever else it takes to make us feel ready.

In the early days as a consultant, my approach was simple. I listened a lot. When my clients started dropping unidentifiable three-letter acronyms into the conversation, I nodded and did my best to stay with the *feeling* of what they were talking about.

Learning more 3-letter acronyms was not going to help me be a better consultant. Getting my MBA was not going to help me be a better catalyst for change. All I needed to do was *be present*. It was not *information* that my clients needed, but *transformation* – and I could not be effective if I got the two confused. Please don't get me wrong. I'm not saying that preparation is a waste of time. It's not. But when due diligence turns into obsessive compulsive behavior that has no correlation to outcomes, you are wasting your time and everyone else's, too.

What I learned during my two-minute drill at Wells Fargo was that 90% of my pre-game process had no correlation to outcomes.

Now What?

Think about a challenge you're facing on the job – an anxiety-provoking task usually preceded by over-preparing. In what ways might you be obsessing? How can you decrease your prep time by 50% and still get the same or better result?

THE SEVEN-LETTER WORD

O K. I admit it. I'm a Scrabble addict – an online Scrabble addict, to be more exact. If there was a *Scrabble Anonymous*, I'd be in it, confessing to my word-conjuring comrades the rush I feel every time I lay down the perfect 32-point word. Fourteen games. That's how many I have going on at any given moment, some with people as far away as South Africa. I've played 3,917 games in the past few years and have won 54% of them.

Methinks I've learned more about life from Scrabble than I did from four years of college. Canterbury Tales? The sonnets of William Shakespeare? How to drink odd vodka concoctions until I passed out? Interesting past-times, for sure, but nowhere near the value of insights I've gleaned from the game invented, 76 years ago, by the little known demi-god, Alfred Mosher Butts.

By my own calculations, I've discovered 114 algorithmic variables to the game, subtle principles of play, point, and counterpoint that need to be considered before making a move. And while chess is considered, by many, to be the more sophisticated game, there are strategically synaptic moments in Scrabble that reveal chess to be little more than Pin the Tail on the Donkey at a fourth grade birthday party.

Like all great games, love affairs, and near-death experiences, there is a defining moment in Scrabble that reigns supreme – one existential, moon howling moment that, metaphorically speaking, I imagine was at least partially responsible for Van Gogh cutting off his ear.

I'm talking about the appearance of a perfect seven-letter word in one's rack that cannot be placed on the board because THERE IS NO PLACE TO PUT IT!

This word – this fabulous, pristine, classic, sacred, mellifluous, God-given word DOES NOT FIT. *It does not fit anywhere.* Either the board is too cluttered, my opponent has sealed off all openings, or it just doesn't connect to anything I see. It just sits there. Unmoving. Zen koan-like. The first word of an acceptance speech I will never give.

So there I am, silent and alone with my perfectly crafted seven-letter word, racking what's left of my brain to find it's perfect home, but there is no home, no home on the range, no home on the board, no home away from home, no nothing.

I see the word, am seized by the word, believe in the word, but cannot move. I cannot lay it down. I've been checkmated and I'm not even playing chess.

This game I play, you see, is playing me – the ancient game of trying to express, the game of giving voice to the void, to say *something* significant before I die. This game that's been played since the beginning of time, long before the first hieroglyph, is a game that will continue being played until the sun burns up.

The rules? There is a board, the board of life – the one you and I must agree on to play. There are pieces. That's you and me and the seven billion other souls on planet Earth. We do our best to play, to lay down our words, our songs, our symphonies, sculptures, moves, causes, works of art, businesses, theories, inventions, hopes, and dreams – praying they will, somehow, *connect*, somehow have *impact*, somehow break open the conspiracy of silence long enough for all the forces of goodness and light inside us to express their unspeakable longing to be seen and heard.

And so, good people of cyberspace and time, by the grace of the compassionate Scrabble gods and the extraordinary luxury of having published this book which you now hold in your hands, I hereby, and with great respect for you and all the logophiles in your life, lay down, in the boardless space below, a small sampling of my still untallied seven-letter words for your diversion and delight. May you find a place to put them. And if you can't or won't, may you savor the fact that they exist at all.

Aeolian. Coaxial. Equinox. Samurai. Jukebox. Dervish. Exotica. Kibbitz. Dazzled. Tamales. Jazzier. Oxidize. Moonlit. Courage. Kumquat. Darshan. Praises.

So What?

Whatever you do for a living, it is highly likely that the "board" you are playing on doesn't seem capable of receiving that fabulous seven-letter word you have in your hand – that soulful, creative, high-value expression of what it is you have to contribute. So be it. Sometimes that's just the way life is. Your task is not to make the board wrong. Not only is that a waste of time, it's a distraction from enjoying the feeling of having that outrageous seven-letter word in the first place. Of course, it's always possible that you are in the wrong job – a job where the board is so cluttered that you have no hope of communicating what you really have to say.

Now What?

What is your version of the seven-letter word? How might you move some tiles on the board of your life until it fits? And if that doesn't work, how can you start a new game?

TOEING THE LINE

As a person infinitely more interested in alchemy than chemistry, not once during my early years as a young entrepreneur did I ever aspire to be sitting in a room with ten middle-aged, overweight chemical salesmen from New Jersey – modern day Willy Lomans driving 100,000 miles each year to call on purchasing agents from Maine to Virginia. This in a heroic attempt to sell more of their company's product and hopefully win the "President's Award," bestowed on the lucky honoree at the company's year-end powwow held in the *Belvedere Room* or the *Bellmore Room* or some other vapidly named meeting space in a modestly priced hotel still trying to figure out how to reduce their high rate of employee turnover.

But that's exactly where I found myself.

Somehow, their boss, my client, a regional manager responsible for convincing upper management that this year was going to be a *banner year* – had gotten my name and asked me if I could help his people get out of the box and increase sales by 20%.

While my more politically correct friends chided me for choosing to work with a chemical company, I had absolutely no problem with my choice. I had long ago made peace with the fact that every business had something wrong with it, no matter their industry or how skillful its PR department.

Unless I wanted to be a potter in Vermont, there was always going to be something unseemly about the corporate marketplace. And besides, I had a wife and two young kids to support.

The morning session with the ten chemical salesmen was all they had hoped it would be – an upbeat opportunity to bond and brainstorm. The ideas were flowing and so was the coffee. Everyone was happy.

During the lunch break, I stayed back to set things up for the afternoon session, one I was planning to begin with a hands on activity that required me to place a 20-foot length of masking tape on the floor, parallel to the entrance, which I proceeded to do without a second thought.

At 1:00 p.m., the time I had asked everyone to be in their seats, the room was still totally empty. Just me and the briefcases they had left behind.

Maybe I had the time wrong.

I looked at my watch. I looked at the clock on the wall. Both of them had the exact same time: 1:00 p.m., the time the afternoon session was supposed to begin. Then I looked at the door. It was open, but all ten of the chemical salesmen were standing, unmoving, *outside* the door in the hallway, as if they were waiting for a bus.

"C'mon in guys," I call. "It's time for the session to begin."

"We can't," they reply.

I walk across the room and ask them why.

In unison, they point to the 20-foot length of tape on the floor.

"Hey, it's OK, guys. It's just a piece of tape."

But they just stand there, looking at me, frozen in time, as if the tape was electrified. As if they were about to do something very wrong. As if they were going to make a BIG MISTAKE they would, somehow, later regret.

So What?

Twenty years later the image of those ten chemical salesmen, convinced they were not allowed to step over the line, is still very much with me. I owe those gentleman an eternal debt of gratitude because they helped me understand a part of the human psyche that I had never seen so dramatically – how the decisions we make about what we can do and what we can't do are often utterly *arbitrary*.

The chemical salesmen interpreted the masking tape on the floor as meaning STOP – their collective generalization of past experiences about lines – unbroken white lines in the middle of a highway, property lines separating neighbor from neighbor, and countless "B" movies where the tough guy draws a line in the sand with a stick and dares anyone to cross it or else.

183

Yes, of course, some lines serve a purpose. I'm glad that the guy driving 75 mph in the oncoming lane doesn't cross the line. But the moment with the chemical salesmen was not the Interstate. It was just a piece of masking tape on the floor. No game was being played. No rules had been set. There was nothing to lose by stepping over it.

One of the primary reasons why innovation remains inert in many organizations is because masses of intelligent, innately creative people are interpreting tape on the floor as lines that cannot be crossed. We are fabricating boundaries where none exist. We are drawing lines in space – lines that separate, isolate, and marginalize. Lines between us and our customers. Lines between the past and the present. Lines between what's possible and what's not. All obstacles are no more than 20-foot lengths of masking tape on the floor. Whether you put them there or someone else puts them there, they have no power other than the power we attribute to them.

Now What?

On an 8 X 11 piece of paper, napkin, or extended stretch of sandy beach, make two columns: Column #1: "20 Foot Pieces of Masking Tape I Haven't Yet Stepped Over" and Column #2: "What I Will Do This Month to Step Over Them." If, having done so, you still aren't inspired to step over the line, contemplate any of the following quotes.

"Don't be afraid to take a big step. You can't cross a chasm in two small jumps."

—David Lloyd George

"Whatever you can do, or dream you can, begin it. Boldness has genius, power and magic in it."

—Goethe

"Security is mostly a superstition. Life is either a daring adventure or nothing."

—Helen Keller

"It's not because things are difficult that we dare not venture. It's because we dare not venture that they are difficult."

—Seneca

"Only those who will risk going too far can possibly find out how far it is possible to go."

—T.S. Eliot

WRITING SPEECHES, SAYING NOTHING

Henry Miller wrote 10,000 pages before any of his words were published. Richard Bach's *Jonathan Livingston Seagull* was rejected 18 times before it went on to sell 60 million copies. Salman Rushdie, after the publication of his *Satanic Verses*, spent a lot of time wearing disguises so he wouldn't be executed by a pissed off Ayatollah Khomeini and an entire nation of Fatwa-obsessed Muslims.

Me? My writer's come-uppance came in the form of a 24-hour ATM at LaGuardia Airport. But first, the back story.

When I was pounding the streets of Denver, Colorado, as an aspiring freelance writer, I once wrote a feature article for the *American Humane Magazine*. The story was well-received and inspired the Executive Editor, Eric Brettschneider, to send me a glowing letter of acknowledgment.

I kept his letter of acknowledgment along with a few others I had received, but since I couldn't *eat* them, I decided to move to New York City in an attempt to reignite my stalled writing career.

The first call I made upon arriving in the Big Apple was to my one and only local fan, Eric Brettschneider.

Eric was not in! In fact, Eric was *never* going to be in, explained the woman who answered the phone. Eric, she went on to say, was no longer with the *American Humane Society*. He had "moved on." Precisely *where* she wasn't at liberty to say, but she *could* give me a forwarding number, which she proceeded to do.

Eric, answering his own phone, remembered me fondly and explained he was now the Executive Assistant to the Borough President of Queens, the Honorable Donald R. Manes.

"Shit," I thought to myself. "Another dead end."

Eric, however, saw it differently.

"Our speechwriter may be leaving next month," he explained. "Why don't you take a shot at writing Donald's State of the Union address? The pay is good and it'll give me a chance to see if you've got the right stuff to be our next speechwriter."

Yes, indeed, the pay *was* good. And so was the feedback. The Honorable Donald R. Manes was pleased with my work and so were the good people of Queens, happy to know that their not yet indicted Borough President had an excellent grasp of all the local issues.

Months passed. I did some brochure writing for Citibank (boring), wrote an article for *New York Magazine* (rejected), and ate a lot of beans (kidney). And then, like an unexpected tax refund from the Great State of New York, the new Executive Assistant to the Borough President of Queens called.

"Good news!" he exclaimed. "Our speechwriter just quit. Come in tomorrow for an interview with Donald if you want the job."

"This," I thought to myself, "is going to be one very short job interview," knowing how pathetically apolitical I was. Yes, I knew that each state had two senators and that jaywalking was illegal, but after that my knowledge of the inner workings of government had some major holes in it. My job interview *was* indeed short. But not in the way I expected. Here's how it went:

1. Eric escorted me to the well-appointed, corner office of the Borough President of Queens.

2. I knocked and the door opened, revealing several American flags and a nicely framed photo of Mario Cuomo.

3. Donald Manes spoke: "Eric tells me you have a good sense of humor. True?"

4. "Yes," I replied.

5. Donald Manes smiled, "Good! You're hired."

That was it! – my initiation into the halls of power. I was *not* grilled about the Federalist Papers, *not* asked about my position on gun control, *not* invited into a dialogue about New York City's budget. *One question.* That's all I was asked – probably the only question I could have answered at the time:

Did I have a sense of humor? Thus began my two-year career as a political speechwriter.

While many soul-sucking experiences happened to me during that particularly surreal time in my life, none of them came close to the existential meltdown I had when I was asked to write a speech about the opening of a 24-hour ATM machine at LaGuardia Airport.

I mean, *really*, what is there to say about that? "Good people of Queens, I am proud and privileged to be standing here with you today, just three feet away from LaGuardia Airport's first-ever Automated Teller Machine."

OK. So a young Albert Einstein once worked in a patent office. Great. I got it. But... this... *THIS*... this speechwriting for a man who rolled up almost every speech I wrote and used it as a *pointer* while he spoke off the cuff?

Was it karma? God's wicked sense of humor? Had I taken a wrong turn off the Queens Expressway of Life?

Like the speechwriter before me and the one before him in a succession of who knows how many going all the way back to Egypt where the scribes were asked to write on the walls of the pyramids just how awesome the pharaohs were for reducing famines by 30%, the drama I found myself in was a timeless one.

The real question wasn't how I got here. The real question was this: *What story was I going to tell about the events taking place in my life* – a story that could easily be interpreted very differently by someone else. Did I need to hunker down and plumb the depths of the experience waiting for me in the Queens

Borough President's office? Or did I simply need to read the ATM on the wall and move on to higher ground?

So What?

Everything we do and every place we go has the potential to be a catalyst for learning and growth. Yes, there are "good jobs" and "bad jobs" and yes, I hope you find the good jobs and stay away from the bad ones, but always, like the alchemists of old, we have the power to turn lead into gold – and if not gold, than at least the silver lining in every situation. In many ways, we learn more from the bad than we do from the good, more from failure than from success. It's all a matter of perspective. I say this not to provide a rationalization for accepting a mediocre job. I say this because the power to extract meaning from anything is built into us – to honor "what is" – to mine the depths of what life has in store for us and to discover the wisdom that is there.

Now What?

Think about your current work situation. Do you love it? If you don't, understand you have three choices: 1) You can quit and find a job you love; 2) You can quit and create a job you love; 3) You can shake things up in your current work situation so that the work you do there is more meaningful. Which path will you take?

STANDING IN THE BACK OF THE BUS

Iam standing in the back of a bus in San Miguel de Allende, just beginning to exit, when I notice a short, heavy-set woman behind me, her long grey hair tied in a bun. She is smiling in a way that explains a thousand years of Mexican fiestas. How could I not let her pass?

So I take a step to the side and, with a downward sweep of my hand, indicate she should pass me – that indeed, it would be my pleasure if she did. And so she does, her eyes opening wider, the many laugh lines around her dark eyes deepening.

I have the impulse to follow, to exit next, especially since I had just given up my place in line, but the boy behind her is obviously on his way somewhere and his need to exit seems to be greater than mine and since I am *already* standing off to the side, I let the young muchacho do his young muchacho thing.

A man with a guitar passes me, as do two small children.

193

I look to my left and see a lot of people starting to make their way to the back of the bus, me now feeling like an usher, perfectly placed to make their exit just a little happier today.

A dark-skinned man with fringes on his jacket passes by, as does a woman behind him whom I imagine to be his wife. She looks tired, like there are many chores waiting for her at home – the same chores her mother and grandmother still perform daily as an act of worship to a Jesus whose image hangs from the rearview mirror of her husband's 1973 Chevy, along with the rosary beads and dice.

Each of these people pass me and, as they do, I notice that *more* people are getting on the bus – the same number, mas o menos, as those who have just gotten off.

So I continue standing there, making way, and nodding to those who seem to be open to more than just a smile. And then, it dawns on me. *This is my work.* This is what I was born for – what my Buddhist friends like to refer to as "right livelihood," though I, in this moment, could not figure out *how* the universe could possibly compensate me for my service.

I didn't need to think about it for long.

Twenty minutes later, a woman with a turquoise barrette in her hair, brings me a grilled chicken in a plastic bag and a 7-Up, perfectly chilled.

So What?

Some of us have found our work in this world. Some have merely found a job. Me? My moment on the back of the bus in San Miguel showed me the difference – that it had nothing to do with money, title, or a 401K and everything to do with *feeling* no matter what we do. Back of the bus? Corner office? C-Suite? It makes no difference. Without the feeling of being fully alive and of service, who cares?

NOW WHAT?

Put money and people's opinions aside for a moment. Then describe what your real work looks like – not next lifetime but in this lifetime. Where are you? What are you doing? How does it make you feel?

THE SOUND OF A VOLKSWAGEN ENGINE

As a ten-year old boy growing up in the suburbs of New York, I had a lot of hidden talents that went largely unnoticed by the people around me – the most unique one being an ability to recognize the sound of a 1961 Volkswagen as it made its way up the tree-lined street outside my bedroom window at midnight. That's when my father, a man far more comfortable in his store than he ever was at home, would return from work – tired, grouchy, and badly in need of someone to listen to his stories of the day. Customers were easy. Family was not – three tax exemptions he had a hard time not treating like employees. I wanted nothing to do with him. He prayed at the altar of work. I prayed at the altar of play. He made my mother cry. I made my mother laugh. Which is why, the moment I heard his Volkswagen chugging up the street, I'd turn off my TV, pull the cord on my lamp, and pretend to be asleep.

Five minutes later he would enter my room, put his hand on the TV, kneel, and put his head on my chest – the stubble from his day's beard penetrating the top of my pajamas. For a moment, he was silent. He could hear, I think, my heart beat. I could hear him breathing. Then he would ask me about my day. I would answer from a world very far away. This would go on for a minute or two. Then he would stand, walk to the window, and open it half way, so I would have fresh air to breathe.

So What?

This story, of course, is only one perspective – mine at ten. I'm sure my father would have told a very different story, scarred, as he was, by the Great Depression, and driven to make sure he earned enough money to send both his children to college so we wouldn't have to work in a rabbit pelt tanning factory, like he did, at 15. First impressions, however, run deep. They are not logical. Seeing my father so worn out by work and gone more often than not convinced me, at an early age, that *work* was the problem. If it took my father away and made him so tired and cranky, how good could it be? Maybe that's why it took me until the age of 40 to start my own business, spooked by the prospect that I would also become a victim of work that I too one day would only be able to talk to my children in the dark.

Now What?

Think about your mother and father for a moment. When you were ten, what was their approach to work? And how much of their approach do you think has affected your current relationship to work?

198

ALMOST DROWNING

When I was 21, living the hippie life on Martha's Vineyard, I invited my new girlfriend, Connie, to spend a day with me on the island's most remote beach – a place only the locals knew about. Having the weekend off from my dishwashing job was a great relief, so I packed a picnic lunch, picked Connie up, and drove to our destination. Life was good. The sun was shining, the sky was blue, and tomorrow was a day off.

After ten minutes of vigorous swimming, I turned to look at Connie, but instead of the smile I expected, I saw only panic in her eyes. Something was wrong. Maybe she had a cramp, I thought, so I swam to her side, placed my hand across her chin and, with my free arm, tried my best to sidestroke both of us to shore – something I had once seen in a movie. It did not work.

Not only wasn't I a strong enough swimmer to pull it off, the tide had turned and was pulling us out to sea. Rip tide!

So I give my girlfriend the "I'm going for help" look and begin swimming as fast as I can – not directly in, but *diagonally* – the only direction I can move. It is hard to raise my arms, hard to stay afloat, and then, an answer to a prayer. There, no more than 20 yards in from of me is a huge rock rising out of the ocean. The current is taking me there! Hallelujah! Finally, a place to rest and catch my breath!

The next thing I know I am spread-eagled on top of the rock and trying to get a grip, but the rock is covered with coral and the coral is covered with algae. A big wave comes and knocks me back into the ocean, but instead of swimming I find myself strangely climbing some kind of invisible ladder. Up I go and then down, my head above the water for a breath, then below, swallowing the sea that is swallowing me. My third time up the ladder, I look to shore and a single thought rushes through my mind.

"You will die here and people will remember you as the person who died here."

This moment, this stark, cold, shocking moment of imminent death, feels like the only real moment I've ever had in my life. Completely alive, I am! Completely awake! And *this* is going to be the last moment of my life. The past 21 years? A cartoon, at best, compared to this.

And then, something far beyond my knowing takes control. It moves my arms and legs. It turns my head. It gulps the air until I find myself in water only knee deep. I stand and stumble to the shore, but there is no one there. No one. The beach is empty. There is not a soul in sight. That's when the only word accessible to me comes flying out of my mouth.

"HELPPP!!!!" I scream to the void. "HEELLLPPP!!" I scream at the top of my lungs.

To my right, I see a woman slowly walking towards me.

"HELLLPPPP!" I scream again, pointing to the ocean so she can see. But there is no one there – no one at all. Only waves… and froth… and foam. It is at this precise moment in time that something, beyond death, dies within me. I am alive, but Connie is not. I cannot believe it. How can this be happening? What in God's name? And then … I see… a head… bobbing above the waves. It's her. Connie. She is alive… treading water… waiting.

A young woman and her boyfriend swim out and bring her in. Then, making sure we're both all right, continue on their way. Connie and I drop to our knees and kiss the ground. The sand is hot. Then, for the next two hours, all we do is sing.

So What?

It's all about perspective, isn't it? When you're going down for the third time, what really matters? Your job? Your career? Your savings account? I don't think so. When you're going down for the third time, the only thing that matters is breath and the impulse to live – the kind of impulse that is so unbelievably primal, you find yourself tapping into a realm of potential you never knew you had – what life is all about: waking all the way up and allowing yourself to be moved by the force that moves all things. A moment of truth? Yes, indeed. The good news is that none of us needs to be on the brink of death to experience it. Anything can awaken it in us. Anything. At 21, I was thickheaded enough, I guess, to have needed this kind of experience to wake me from my dream. But that's my story, not yours. Your wake up call can happen *today* in a thousand different ways. And maybe, just maybe, this little story of mine will bring you closer to the shore.

Now What?

Imagine you have only a few seconds left to live. Imagine you are going down for the third time. What would be important to you? What would you care about? Whatever that is, focus on it now. Cherish it. Savor it. Give it everything you have. None of us know when our last few seconds will come.

THE ART AND SCIENCE OF STORYTELLING

Entering the Realm
of the Evocative

"There have been great societies that did not use the wheel,
but there have been no societies that did not tell stories."

—Ursula K. Le Guin

A good story, like good perfume, is evocative. Listening
to it calls forth a response that moves a person from
one state of mind to another – not just for the moment, but for all
time, because a well-told story is long remembered. What moves
inside the listener not only follows the arc of the story, but also
opens the listener to a space of discovery.

Music is a perfect example. A good piece of music is
composed of at least as many pauses as notes. Indeed, it is the
spaces *between* the notes that evoke feeling, allowing the listener
to deeply experience something beyond time.

Amateur composers sometimes do too much, cluttering their creations with themselves, making the music more about their own proficiency than the depth of what's possible to evoke in others – a phenomenon that led jazz-great, Dizzy Gillespie, to confess, "It took me my entire life to learn what not to play."

The same holds true with story. The skillful storyteller doesn't tell too much, doesn't clutter the tale with his telling. Instead, he provides just enough detail for the listener to enter his world and *participate*. That's the goal of any work of art – to create a space for people to explore new realms.

Ultimately, the storyteller's task is a simple one – *to create the stage for the human heart to dance* – what hearing a cello in the distance does to you at dusk or how you feel upon opening a love letter.

WHAT'S THE STORY WITH STORY?

"Inside each of us is a natural born storyteller just waiting to be released."

—Robin Moore

The roots of the word *story*, most commonly defined as a "connected account or narration of some happening," can be traced back to three sources:

1. The 12th century Old French word *estoire*, meaning "a chronicle or history";

2. The Late Latin word *storia*, meaning "history, account, or tale," and

3. The Greek word *historia* meaning "an account of one's inquiries."

All three sources share one thing in common – that "story" is a linguistic creation of a human being's attempt to give an account of "what happened."

When we make sense of the events in our lives, we call it *story*. When civilizations do this it's called *history*. Both are two sides of the same coin – the attempt to give shape to a series of events over time.

How true our stories or histories are depends on who is telling them, plus their motivations, perceptions, and sources of information. The advertising industry, for example, constructs its narratives with only one thing in mind – to increase the odds of consumers buying specific goods – a goal that explains why the general public, in the 1950's, came to believe that smoking cigarettes was actually a healthy thing to do.

The same phenomenon holds true for the news industry, lobbyists, political spin-doctors, publicists, futurists, salesmen, and teenagers attempting to explain to their parents why they need to text 250 times a day. Everyone has a point of view. And everyone is doing what they can to construct their stories in a way that has the greatest influence on others.

That's what any parent who has ever told his child a fairy tale has done – toggling back and forth between trying to impart timeless values and getting the little one to fall asleep.

No matter what the storyteller's intention, all accounts of what has happened have the same purpose – to influence others. Whether the end game is enlightenment, entertainment, deception, or getting out of a speeding ticket, there is no denying that story is our species preferred method for communicating meaning.

WHY TELL STORIES?

"Stories make us more alive, more human, more courageous, more loving."

—Madeleine L'Engle

In the last 60 seconds, here's what's happened: 168 million emails were sent, 700,000 Google searches were launched, and 60 hours of YouTube videos were uploaded, not to mention all the spam, banner ads, phone calls, Facebook posts, tweets, texts, memos, and telemarketing calls.

A whopping 90% of all data in the world has been generated in the past two years alone. Before the dawn of civilization, approximately 5 exabytes of information was created. Now, that much information is created every two days.

The common term for this head-spinning phenomenon is "information overload" – the inability to process all the information we are exposed to. And while the gory statistics change every nanosecond, the results are the same, often leading to what is now referred to as "Information Fatigue Syndrome" (IFS) – a condition with symptoms that include poor concentration, depression, burnout, hostility, compulsive checking of social media, and falling into trance-like states.

This describes the mindset of many of the people you are attempting to influence, whether customers, clients, friends, voters, volunteers, government officials, patients, readers, or potential soul-mates.

If you are committed to delivering a meaningful, memorable message to another human being, the burning question you need to be asking is: "How can I cut through the background noise of the marketplace so my message can be heard and remembered?"

According to communication experts of all kinds, the answer is simple: *storytelling*.

Storytelling is the most effective, time-tested, dependable way of transmitting meaning from one human being to another. It's been going on since the beginning of time when our first ancestors stood around the tribal fire. It's how civilizations pass on their wisdom to the next generation. It's how religions pass on the sacred teachings of their faith. And it's how parents transmit the values they want to impart to their children.

Here are just a few of the reasons why storytelling is so powerful:

It quickly establishes trust and connection between the speaker and listener. It increases receptivity, captures attention, engages emotions, and allows the receiver to participate in the narrative. It communicates values, not just skills, decreases teaching time, builds community, and ignites five more regions of the brain than mere fact-giving. It also helps people make sense of their world, shapes perceptions via the subconscious mind, reframes frustration, paradox, and suffering; changes behavior, and provides a way for people to remember, retrieve, and retell a meaningful message.

Think about a message you want to communicate to someone today. How might you do that by telling a *story*, instead of overloading them with information, statistics, and pep talks?

TUNING INTO MOMENTS OF TRUTH

"The shortest distance between a human being and the truth is a story."
—Anthony de Mello

As the story goes, 2,500 years ago, Buddha gave a wordless sermon to his disciples. All he did was to hold up a single white flower – a lotus. That's it. No words. Just a flower. All his disciples were mystified, except, that is, Mahakasyapa, a young monk who immediately smiled, signifying the direct transmission of wisdom from Master to student – a moment referred to in Buddhist literature as "tathagata," the ineffable nature of *suchness.*

Something within Mahakasyapa instantly understood the non-verbal essence of Buddha's communication to him. *He got it in a flash.* No thought was necessary, no analysis, no intellectualization. It was as if a veil had lifted and he experienced something profound that had previously been inaccessible to him.

Let's call the young monk's recognition a "moment of truth".

The good news for the rest of us is that a person does not need to be a monk to experience a moment of truth. Nor must all moments of truth be "spiritual" or historically significant. Moments of truth are for everyone and they come in all varieties – small, medium, and large – spontaneously occurring, unplanned *happenings* that have, embedded within them, the potential for great learning, insight, and wisdom. Simply put, a kind of Red Sea parts and a meaningful lesson is learned, even if no teacher is present. We all have them, but like dreams they are easy to forget, dismiss, or undervalue.

The catalyst for a moment of truth can be anything. For the young monk, it was a flower. For me, it was poached eggs, arm wrestling a CIA agent, listening to an Afghani cab driver's story, and a truckload of other triggers noted in this book. For *you*, who knows? An unexpected promotion? Missing a train? A glance from a beggar? Getting fired? A divorce? Almost dying? A blues song? It doesn't matter *what*, as long as it sparks an inner shift that moves you beyond old assumptions and outdated beliefs to experience the magic of life in a new way.

If you deconstruct the stories we tell, you'll discover that most of them turn out to be our attempts to give shape to these moments of truth – our verbal deciphering of a moment in time (or outside of time) that had great significance for us, even if that moment is invisible to others.

Unspoken, these moments of truth remain hidden, buried inside us like treasure. Expressed, they uplift, inspire, and empower.

THE FINE ART OF
CONNECTING THE DOTS

"It has been said that next to hunger and thirst, our most basic human need is for storytelling."

—Khalil Gibran

I remember as a small child playing a game called "Connect the Dots." In front of me was an activities book composed of sheets of paper with nothing on them but numbered dots. My task was a simple one – to draw lines between the dots, connecting each dot sequentially. #1 would connect to #2. #2 would connect to #3 and so on until all of the dots were connected. This created some kind of picture — a hat, a house, a boat, or whatever the book publisher had in mind. I found this fascinating, thrilled that out of nothing something would emerge. And while I did not grow up to become an artist, I did develop an interest in the phenomenon of pattern recognition, pattern making, and the various ways in which human beings construct their own reality.

As I got older, it became clear to me that this same children's game of connecting the dots had played itself out in many ways throughout human history. Who drew the constellations if not bigger kids, the ancient Greeks and Babylonians, connecting non-numbered dots in the night sky – the product of their need to make sense out of what they saw. And so Orion, Canis Major, the Big Dipper, and 84 other configurations of stars came into being – points of light clustered and named by the earth's first farmers to help them figure out when to plant and when to harvest. And to help *remember* the constellations, these same farmers made up myths – stories they could pass on to the next generation to remind them of the patterns in the sky.

But it wasn't only farmers who benefitted from this connecting the dots, myth-making phenomenon. Ancient sailors did too – adventurers who navigated their journeys across unchartered seas by watching the skies to mark their positions, constellations drawn by human beings who connected the dots.

That's what we do. *We connect the dots.* We make patterns. And then we translate what we see into story to remember and communicate what we see. First there is a point – an isolated moment in time (and space) when something becomes perceivable – a leaf falling, a dog barking, a point of light. In and of itself, this perceptible "thing" is just an isolated dot. In the first instant when it becomes known to the observer, it is freestanding and unrelated to anything else. It is not connected to the past or the future. It is not the beginning of something or the end of something. There is no plot, no unfolding of events, no Act One, Scene Two. *It just is.*

But soon the story-making part of our mind kicks in – the constellation maker. It begins to make sense of what we see. We draw invisible lines through time and space until a picture emerges to help us make sense of our experience. Standing beneath the infinite sky of possibilities, this pattern-making tendency brings orientation, comfort, and a newfound ability to communicate our experience to others.

The most dramatic examples of this are the *creation myths* – the symbolic narratives of how the world began and how people first came to inhabit it. Every culture has its own – elaborate cosmological stories with plot and characters and a healthy dose of deities.

Deconstruct any scripture and you will find that its DNA is *story* – parables, allegories, and tales that have become the human shorthand for delivering meaningful, memorable messages upon which we base our lives.

Now, here's where it gets really interesting. When the dots are numbered and we proceed to connect them in the same, sequential progression, we always arrive at the same picture – conclusions that everyone can agree on. But when the dots are *not* numbered and the dot connectors (that's us) realize we have a choice about how we connect them and whether to make the lines, wiggly, wavy, or straight, a very different picture emerges and a very different story unfolds.

The simplest example of this is a husband and wife arguing. While the same dots may be marked on the paper, the way in which the husband and wife connect the dots is different. He sees it one way. She sees it the other. The result? The plot of many a modern-day sitcom and a 50% divorce rate.

This phenomenon plays out on many other stages as well. The Israelis, for example, connect the dots differently than the Palestinians. Virgos connect the dots differently than Leos. And the Native Americans connect the dots differently than America's so-called, "Founding Fathers." The story told in all three situations? Very different.

Psychologists attribute our dot-connecting behavior to a cognitive principle they have reduced to three words: "Motivation affects perception." We see, they say, what we are primed to see, filtered through our need or desire of the moment – a phenomenon that Eastern pundits have translated in their own, more metaphorical way, "When a pickpocket meets a saint, all he sees are pockets."

Done well, storytelling is a force for good, an extraordinary means to energize, uplift, inspire, and transmit wisdom. Abused, storytelling yields an entirely different result. Con artists, for example, tell very believable stories, but only with the intention to deceive. The same goes for corrupt politicians, cheating spouses, warmongers, the sensationalist media, gossipers, most of the advertising world, and anyone else attempting to bend the truth for their own personal gain.

The fact that human beings are story-making machines is undebatable. From the first Paleolithic cave paintings to the latest Hollywood blockbusters, that's what we do. What's up for grabs is this: the kind of stories we choose to tell.

WHAT IS WISDOM? WHO IS WISE?

"Modern storytellers are the descendants of an immense and ancient community of holy people, troubadours, bards, griots, cantadoras, cantors, traveling poets, bums, hags, and crazy people."

—Clarissa Pinkola Estés

In the world today, there are 6,500 spoken languages, 4,200 religions, 196 countries, 31 kinds of government, 12 astrological signs, and 5 major branches of philosophy – all indicators of the extraordinary diversity of the human race. But there is only one name for the people who experience this diversity – "homo sapiens."

Homo sapiens, the scientific name for our species, originates from the Latin "homo" (human being) and "sapiens" (wise). Our name, simply put, means "wise human being." It is *wisdom*, or at least the *capacity* for wisdom, that all human beings share.

Wisdom is not just theoretical knowledge or a collection of philosophical insights. It is the ability to perform an action with the highest degree of adequacy under any given circumstance. Wisdom implies a possession of knowledge and awareness that, *when applied* to a given situation, ensures the best possible outcome. "Truth in action," you might say.

A classic example of wisdom is known as the "Judgment of Solomon." As the story goes, two women came to Solomon to resolve a quarrel over who was the true mother of a particular baby. When Solomon suggested they should divide the child in two with a sword, one woman said she would rather give up the child than see it killed. Solomon then declared the woman who showed compassion to be the true mother and gave the baby to her.

A modern day example of wisdom can be found in the musical *Fiddler on the Roof*. Two men in the town square are arguing over a recent business transaction. The buyer claims that the horse he bought from the seller was actually a mule, while the seller loudly proclaims that the animal is, in fact, a horse. Back and forth they argue, each making his case, getting louder and louder by the minute, when finally they see Tevyev, the town milkman, walking nearby. Calling him over, the buyer makes a case for why the animal he bought is *not* a horse, but a mule. Tevyev listens carefully, strokes his beard, and declares, "You're right!" The seller, aghast at Tevyev's judgment, proceeds to make *his* case for why the animal is indeed, a horse, and *not* a mule. Tevyev listens carefully, strokes his beard, and again declares, "You're right!" Meanwhile, a neutral observer, who has been closely watching the heated exchange, steps forward, turns to

Tevyev and blurts: "Wait a minute, Tevyev! How can *he* (pointing to the buyer) and *he* (pointing to the seller) both be right?" Tevyev listens carefully, strokes his beard, and declares, "You're right!" Then he starts dancing ecstatically.

I realize, of course, that if you are a lawyer or a breeder of horses or mules, Tevyev's answer may not satisfy you, but at another level, his answer was brilliant, addressing an issue at the root of a deeper, unexpressed conflict – *self-righteousness* and the tendency we humans have to draw conclusions based on limited perceptions, circumstantial evidence, and our individual desire for a specific outcome.

If you study the literature of the world's spiritual traditions, you will find that *story* is often the preferred medium for communicating wisdom – non-didactic teachings that penetrate the reader/listener and spark insight, awareness, and the kind of meaning that can easily be remembered and retold to others.

For example, I could have chosen to read and summarize the 293,000,000 articles I found when doing a Google search on "wisdom," *or* I could have told you two simple stories – the Solomon story and the *Fiddler on the Roof* story. The first approach would have taken a very long time and you would have probably experienced it as just another overwhelming download of conceptual knowledge. The second approach, *the story approach*, cut to the chase in less than two minutes and will probably be remembered for the rest of your life.

STORY AS THE TROJAN HORSE
OF WISDOM

"Storytelling reveals meaning without committing the error of defining it."

—Hannah Arendt

Most people, at sometime in their life, enter into a period of "seeking." The language they use to describe their goals may be different, but the intention is the same – to tap into a higher dimension of knowing and become self-realized. The specific form this questing takes varies. Some people go on pilgrimages, some go to mountaintops or caves, some spend time in nature, join monasteries, read holy books, meditate, practice yoga, or search for a Great Teacher.

The underlying assumption of all these seeking strategies is the same. "There is something I don't know. There is something I've not yet experienced. There is a deep wisdom I need to find."

And so begins the hero's journey. Or the heroine's.

And while this seeking sometimes leads to the kind of awakening the Great Masters have been talking about since the beginning of time, I believe there is a complementary, start-where-you-are strategy that also deserves consideration – not to replace the classic quest for Knowledge, but to help the seeker understand that he or she *already* has a lot of the wisdom they are seeking. It's just hidden.

It's hiding in story, those magical, memorable, tellable moments that have already happened to you – times when the light went on, you felt something deeply and connected with a timeless truth even if the catalyst for that experience was mundane or unheroic.

Story is the Trojan Horse of wisdom, the shape our life lessons take, the container for all the clues we need to wake up and live a conscious, loving, powerful, courageous, soulful, creative, fulfilled life. But until we open this Trojan Horse's "trap door" much of this potential remains inaccessible to us.

It's like the classic story of the poor farmer and his wife. Every day they worked the fields from dawn to dusk. Every night for dinner they ate boiled potato skins and shivered in the cold under the only threadbare blanket they could afford. Then one day the builder of their house stopped by, invited them into the kitchen, and lifted a loose floorboard to reveal a bag of gold, which he then bestowed upon the farmer and his wife. For 50 years, they had been walking above it, never more than a few inches from it, living their lives in abject poverty. But now they were rich.

If you like, think of your journey into the power of story as a lifting of the floorboard. What you will discover is that you have *already* learned a lot on the path of life. Now all you need to do is reach in and grab those stories, explore the treasures within and share them with others. Not only will you benefit, but also so will everyone else who has the privilege of hearing them.

It's a revolution of storytelling that's being launched, folks – each of us coming out of our closets to share what we've learned – not to preach, explain, impress, manipulate, educate, or bend others to our will, but to fan the flames of wisdom in a world that sorely needs it.

THE SECRET CODE OF
TACIT KNOWLEDGE

"A story is a way to say something that can be said no other way."
—Flannery O'Connor

What is it that all human beings share in common other than the need for air, water, and the fact that they will answer this question in a wide variety of ways? *A deeply ingrained need to know.*

For some of us, this knowledge-seeking impulse revolves around *survival* – how to grow food, create shelter, and avoid being eaten by the nearest predator. For others, this drive takes the shape of more esoteric knowing – understanding how the universe works, for example, or how to make a killing in the world of credit default swaps. For others with more of a spiritual bent, it might take the shape of "knowing God" or "knowing the Self."

Regardless of the knowledge-seeking realm that drives us, all three groups share one thing in common – and that is a *thirst to understand something they don't yet understand* – an insight, know-how, or wisdom they believe will add more value to their lives.

If this impulse towards knowing is indeed universal, then the question we need to be asking ourselves is: "*What is the most effective way to obtain the knowledge we seek?*" How do we learn what we don't yet know?

Traditional knowledge seekers answer this question in predicable ways – an approach that usually frames the missing knowledge as a commodity that can be secured. "*Ask someone who knows,*" might be one person's approach. Or "*read a book...* or *take a class*"... or, more recently, "*Google it*" – the common assumption being that our missing knowledge is codified somewhere and can be communicated in an immediately transferrable way. And while there are definite benefits to this kind of *explicit knowledge transfer,* this approach is inherently flawed, given the fact that there are many things to learn that cannot be learned this way.

Riding a bicycle, for example, is more easily learned by *observing* somebody riding a bicycle and then *getting on* one than it is by reading a book about the physics of bike movement. The same holds true for learning a language or kneading dough – neither of which can be mastered by reading a list of instructions. Each of these activities requires a transfer of tacit knowledge –

the difficult-to-describe, intuitive, experience-based wisdom from someone "in the know."

It was Michael Polanyi, in 1958, via his magnum opus, *Personal Knowledge*, who first introduced the concept of "tacit knowledge" to the Western world – his attempt to communicate that "we know more than we can tell," and that this knowing requires extensive, ongoing, personal contact with "people in the know," respect for pre-logical knowing, practice, and a healthy dose of trust. Some years later, Japanese organizational theorist, Ikujiro Nonaka, added his take on the matter, applying the tenets of tacit knowledge to the now growing field of knowledge management.

Whereas science is "know why" and networking is "know who," *tacit knowledge* is "know how" – how homo sapiens transfer what they know to others in the most elegant, effortless, and effective way possible.

These days, as technology escalates, markets shift, and employee turnover increases, many forward-thinking companies are doing what they can to codify their knowledge, building sophisticated software and knowledge management systems to ensure the ongoing transmission of know how within their enterprises. And while their attempts are laudable, the fact remains that the transfer of tacit knowledge remains difficult to capture.

What does all of this have to do with storytelling? A lot. Because *story* remains one of the best ways human beings have discovered to communicate the essence of what they know and value. And while it's true that *tacit knowledge* can never be 100% codified, *story* is *know how's* closest surrogate.

If you want to increase the amount of tacit knowledge transfer in your organization, here are four simple ways to begin:

1. Conduct and distribute interviews with your organization's tacit knowledge keepers.

2. Create opportunities for people to observe and apprentice with your organization's tacit knowledge keepers.

3. Record, distribute, and tell organizational stories that communicate key insights.

4. Initiate more hands-on action learning (where doing replaces rote learning.)

THE ART OF LISTENING

*"Most of the successful people I know are the ones who do
more listening than talking."*
—Bernard Baruch

The most important thing you need in order to tell a
good story is not a plot, setting, characters, conflict,
or resolution. The most important thing you need is *someone to
tell*. But not just *any* someone. Someone who is *listening*. A story
without a listener is like a tree in the proverbial forest. If it falls
and there is no one to hear, does it really make a sound?

If there is going to be a storytelling revolution in the world,
there first must be a *listening* revolution – and you, my friend, are
on the front lines.

Real listening is not a pause in conversation in which you
impatiently wait for the other person to finish so you can have
your say. That is not listening. That is *conversational endurance*.

Real listening is what happens when you are fully present, curious, free of your own agendas, respectful, and open to the possibility that the speaker may actually have something of value to share with you. *Receiving*, not *sending*, is what it's all about.

Real listening is a gift we can give each other and it is absolutely free. The only thing we need to pay is our *attention*. Like an incubator, it establishes the conditions conducive to growth. The more you listen, the deeper the storyteller will dive and the more they will surface with the kind of content that will be meaningful to you.

Out of practice? No problem. The following guidelines will get you back on track.

1. When someone begins telling you a story, get curious. If you don't have the time to listen at that moment, schedule another time later.

2. Make eye contact with the storyteller. Nod, smile, or grunt, as inspired.

3. If thoughts or judgments come to mind, choose not to entertain them.

4. Focus! Remember, hearing and listening are two different things.

5. Acknowledge the possibility that, embedded in the story you are being told, is a timely message – one that will energize, awaken, and reveal.

6. If you've already heard the story before, continue listening. Like a good piece of music or a fine piece of art, a good story sustains its value over time.

7. When the storyteller has finished, acknowledge him or her and, if their story resonates with you, express your appreciation.

WHAT TEENAGERS CAN TEACH US ABOUT STORYTELLING

"In my life, the stories I have heard from my family, my friends, my community, and from willing strangers all over the world have been the true source of my education."
—Holly Near

There are approximately 16,000,000 teenage girls living in America. One of them lives in my house. That would be my daughter, Mimi, an extraordinary 18-year old who, shall we say, has given me quite an education.

If you have a teenage daughter, you know what I mean. If you've *been* a teenage daughter, you know what I mean. If you have a friend with a teenage daughter (and spent hours chanting, "It's just a phase she's going through"), you know what I mean. Everyone else – oh ye of no teenagers in your life, please give me the benefit of the doubt for the moment while I shed some light

239

on the little understood science of how to communicate with a teenage girl.

Most people who know me would assume I'd have no trouble communicating with my teenage daughter. I'm smart. I'm laid back and usually thought of as "cool." I am also a professional communicator – my work taking me all over the world to speak with all kinds of people: rocket scientists, computer programmers, college students, actuaries, polymer chemists, PR wizards, cultural creatives, Hollywood executives, video game makers, and everybody else in between.

Compared to communicating with my teenage daughter, these people are a piece of cake.

Usually, my daughter perceives my attempts to engage her in meaningful conversation as lame. I ask what I consider to be authentic, thoughtful questions and, more often than not, receive only inscrutable, one word answers – "Fine," "Good," and "OK" being the most popular.

If I try to be clever in my conversation-opening mode, I succeed only in getting "the look" – the non-verbal equivalent of "I see through your little game of trying to have a conversation with me, Dad, and, God, why would I want to talk with anyone as old as you when, in fact, I have some serious texting to do?"

But today... ah, today... driving Ms. Mimi to school was a Red Sea-parting experience – one of those Archimedes-in-the-bathtub moments we've all heard about.

Are you ready for the secret to communicating to a teenage girl? STORY! Yes, story! Today, instead of my pitiful, Socraticallyinfused, semi-desperate attempt to engage my still-not-yet-fully-formed-frontal-cortex-challenged daughter, I shifted gears. I took a left turn, instead of a right, segueing from something she said to the spontaneous telling of a personal story – the passionate, no-holds-barred account of a life-changing moment that happened to me five years ago in Australia.

I was not probing. I was not teaching. I was not looking for an opening to establish rapport. I was merely recounting a story that mattered to me – one, it turns out, that mattered to *her*, an edgy, aspiring artist who, like me, sometimes also wrestles with doubt.

When the story was over, my daughter was not only fully present, engaged, and responsive, she was asking *me* questions. Here in this space, Mimi and I were one, members of the same tribe sitting around the same fire, the light in each others' eyes all we needed to find our way home.

While there probably aren't a whole lot of teenage girls in your life right now, you, as a human being, entrepreneur, artist, worker bee, business owner, or freelancer are likely faced with the same challenge that millions of parents of teenage girls are faced with. Story can bridge the gap between you and that other person... story connects... story engages in a way that works – the convertible, low-carbon emission vehicle that allows you to travel vast distances between others who may be very different than you. Story is the universally understood medium that makes it profoundly easy to deliver and receive a message, in the least amount of time – one that is empowering, inspiring, and memorable.

HOW TO TELL A GOOD STORY

"Think of story as a mnemonic device for complex ideas."
—Annette Simmons

L et's start with the basics: You already know how to tell a good story. You do. You've been telling good stories your entire life. Today, you've probably told a few. And later, tonight, you will probably tell some more – whether they are merely accounts of your day, a memorable encounter you had at work, or a reminiscence from days gone by.

Story is the ocean we are swimming in. And because it is, we don't necessarily feel wet when we're in it, but we are. Fish aren't taught to swim. And you aren't taught to tell stories. As a child, you didn't need to be taught. All you needed was to hear them and then tell them to others– which you did – everything from The Three Little Pigs… to Jack and the Beanstalk… to the excuses you laid on your teachers for not handing in your homework on time.

Of course, if you had to teach someone how to tell a story in the next ten minutes, you would probably resist because you don't necessarily know how you do it. But just because you don't know how you do it, doesn't mean you lack the knowledge or the skill. You don't. It's in there. It is.

Storytelling is what psychologists refer to as an "unconscious competence" – a skill, like walking, eating, or complaining that has become second nature to you. It's in your bones and has been since you were very young. And while you may not be as skillful as Garrison Keillor, you don't need to be a Garrison Keillor in order to be a good storyteller. In fact, you don't want to be Garrison Keillor. You want to be yourself. Because being yourself is one of the secrets to being a good storyteller.

Where do you begin? With one simple commitment: To stop telling yourself the story that you don't know how to tell a good story.

There is only one thing you need to know if you want to tell a good story: Storytelling is part art and part science. And of the two, it's more about the art than it is about the science.

Communicating your humanity is the art. The more human you are willing to be – that is, not perfect, not an expert, not a superhero – the more likely it is that people will connect with your story.

The key to communicating your humanity? Your passion for telling your story, your respect for your audience, your authenticity, your understanding that people will get what they need without you teaching or preaching, and your ability to engage the attention of others. How to engage and hold attention is an ability that includes seven factors: voice tonality, body language, facial gestures, hand movement, pacing, adapting to the non-verbal cues from your audience, and the choice of which details to include.

Can these be learned? Of course they can. But the real key to successful storytelling is less about study than it is about practice. The more stories you tell, the better you'll get. It's as simple as that. Real-time, you'll figure out what works and what doesn't.

The science of telling a good story is much less complicated than you think. Fundamentally, it's all about structure and the inter-relationships of the elements that comprise the structure. Just like a house needs a foundation, framing, walls, and a roof, a story needs structure too. Once you understand the elements of story structure, you're halfway home. These are:

1. Setting (where your story takes place)

2. Character (the protagonist who has adventures)

3. Plot (the events that unfold – the arc of what happens)

4. Conflict (the obstacles that the characters encounter)

5. Theme (the resolution of the conflict – what's been learned along the way)

How To Discover the Stories You Want To Tell

"The most important question to ask is: What myth am I living?"

—Carl Jung

No matter what your age, a lot has happened to you in this lifetime – the good, the bad, and the ugly – finding love, losing love, being hired, being fired, overcoming obstacles, falling on your face, births, deaths, victories, failures, and everything else in between. Choosing which of this stuff to tell as *story* presents an interesting challenge. The good news is there are many ways to make that choice.

ACKNOWLEDGE THE STORIES YOU ALREADY TELL: All of us have favorite stories we tell – often, more than once. Even if you don't consider yourself a storyteller, there's a good chance you have recounted some of your life experiences to others – people you trusted, loved, or wanted to communicate something meaningful to. Maybe it was your parents, sister, best friend, client, teammate, neighbor, doctor, spouse, or local bartender. Every time you tell one of them the story, he or she listens. What are those stories?

CHUNK OUT THE MAIN EVENTS IN YOUR LIFE: If you were about to die and your life was flashing before your eyes, what would be the key scenes you would see? Growing up in your parent's house? Your first day of school? Falling in love for the first time? The birth of a child? The death of a loved one? Seeing a UFO? Deciding to quit your job? Moving to a foreign country? What else?

IDENTIFY UNEXPECTED MOMENTS OF TRUTH: All of us have experiences that are unplanned – surprise occurrences that challenge our sense of self, blow our minds, and teach us important lessons. Sometimes, all it takes is a trigger phrase to remember them. Take a few minutes now to review the following phrases and notice which stories they spark for you • Overcoming an obstacle • Trusting your gut • Adapting to change • Getting help from an unlikely source • An embarrassing moment • Rising to the occasion • Discovering a hidden talent • Extreme patience • A random act of kindness • Going beyond the call of duty • Being rescued • An unlikely synchronicity • Emerging victorious against all odds • A powerful spiritual experience • Making a difficult choice • Letting go

CHOOSE A WORD AND IDENTIFY STORY IT TRIGGERS:

Faith • Courage • Intuition • Resourcefulness • Creativity Collaboration • Flexibility • Perseverance • Paradox • Celebration Immersion • Surprise • Love • Focus • Intention • Community Paranormal • Magic • Truth • Dream Playfulness • Fear Compassion • Learning • Ritual • Sleep • Holiday • Overtime Proposal • Follow-up • Listening • Music • Loss • Connection

Now, jot down the titles of at least three stories that have come to mind as a result of this little exercise. Then circle the one you most want to tell.

WHAT KIND OF STORIES WILL YOU TELL?

"If history were taught in the form of stories, it would never be forgotten."
—Rudyard Kipling

Here's a story you can probably relate to:

You are walking down a street when a friend, coming the other way, stops, looks you in the eye, and asks "Whassup?" It's a question you've heard a thousand times before – the default, open-ended salutation. Your choices are many. You can answer any way you want, from the predictable, "Fine, whassup with you?" to an elaborate monologue on any number of topics: the weather, upcoming vacation plans, the economy, the latest terrorist attack, local politics, your job, or the high price of cappuccino. In that moment, there is no correct answer. You get to decide what story to tell. What you *don't* get to decide is

251

the impact your story will have. Know this: your story *will* have impact. Everything you say, everything you do has impact, even a seemingly casual moment of passing a friend on the street.

If you watch TV, you can see this phenomenon playing out daily. With an almost infinite number of topics to select from, TV reports are mostly bad news: war, violence, political unrest, terrorism, famine, corruption, plane crashes, murder, scandal, disease, gossip, and unemployment – with an occasional human interest story thrown in for good measure. Sixty-eight percent of Americans believe that TV news broadcasts focus way too much on bad news and yet we keep tuning in. The impact? Our state of well-being declines. We become saddened, more negative, more hopeless and depressed, exacerbating whatever personal worries and anxieties we already had before tuning in.

I'm not suggesting that news outlets airbrush the negative out of their reports. Nor am I suggesting they stop reporting on the bad stuff that is happening. What I'm suggesting is they find more of a middle path and make more of an effort to change the narrative to honor what's good and holy about being alive.

You and I are also news stations. You and I are also reporting on what's going on in the world. Like the TV executives behind the scenes, we also get to decide which stories to tell – even on the street when a friend asks us, "Whassup?" That is our moment of truth. That is our broadcast. Will our stories be local versions of the nightly news, skewed to what's bad and wrong, full of gossip and complaint, or will we choose to tell a *new* story, one infused with possibility, progress, insight, awareness, and hope?

HOW TO FACILITATE
STORYTELLING CIRCLES

"Become aware of what is in you. Announce it, pronounce it, produce it and give birth to it."
—Meister Eckhart

If you are intrigued by the notion of sparking more storytelling in the world, what follows is a simple way to get started. You do not need to be an experienced facilitator to do this nor do you need to be a great storyteller. All you need is an appreciation for story, a love for people, and willingness to stretch your wings. Facilitating storytelling circles is simple because everyone already knows how to tell stories, even if they don't think they know.

Your job is to create the container for storytelling to take shape. There is no one right way to do it. There are many ways. In time, you will find your way. The key is to be authentic, enjoy the process, and be willing to learn from experience. So, here goes, both preparation and facilitation in ten guidelines to get you started.

A. PREPARATION

1. *Create a compelling invitation:* Very few people have ever been invited to a "storytelling circle" (or whatever you end up calling it). Consequently, they have no idea what it is. Your job is to create an invitation that is clear and compelling.

2. *Choose a conducive meeting space:* Storytelling Circles can happen anywhere. But wherever you have one, be sure the space is comfortable, private, and suitable for people to listen, focus, and feel at ease. A circle of chairs is usually a good way to set up the room.

3. *Keep it small:* While the size of the group is up to you, it is advisable to limit the group size to ten or less. This creates a sense of intimacy and increases the odds that a sizable percentage of the group will get a chance to share their stories.

B. FACILITATION

4. *Start the gathering with drinks and snacks:* Whatever you can do to communicate a feeling of ease and welcome is a good thing. One of the simplest ways to do this is to set up a table with finger foods and drinks. This creates a feeling of a community gathering, not a seminar or class.

5. *Explain the purpose and the ground rules:* After everyone is seated, begin by welcoming everyone, introducing

yourself, explaining your role, and restating the purpose of the gathering, that is, to share stories and learn from each other in a relaxed way. Be sure to let people know when the session will end and what the ground rules are:

- Listen with respect

- Be fully present

- Participation is voluntary (nobody is required to tell a story)

- No cell phone usage

- No therapizing, criticizing, or preaching

- Maintain confidentiality (what's said in the room stays in the room)

- Allow you to facilitate

6. **YOU begin the storytelling:** After the ground rules have been communicated (and agreed upon), you tell the first story to get things rolling. Keep your story to four minutes or less and be mindful not to be too theatrical or a "storyteller superhero," which will only intimidate the group and make it less likely for anyone else to step up and tell his or her story.

7. *Engage the group after telling your story:* When you finish telling your story, ask the group to respond to any (or all) of the following questions. Allow no more than ten minutes for this reflection, so you leave ample time for others to tell their stories later.

- What aspects of my story touched or moved you?

- What do you think the key themes of my story are?

- Can any of you relate to my story? If so, in what way?

8. ***Open up the storytelling process to the rest of the group:*** After you've told your "prime the pump" story and the group has had a chance to respond, ask "Who would like to go next?" Remind them of the four-minute storytelling time limit and that you will facilitate the group response to the next story told.

9. ***Continue the storytelling process:*** After the second story has been told and the group has interacted, open up the floor to the third story and the fourth and so on, but be mindful of the time and the group energy. There is no need for everyone to tell a story. In fact, too many stories may overload the group. If people are engaged and inspired to go beyond the agreed upon time limit, check in and ask if they want to extend the session for another set number of minutes.

10. ***Establish mindful closure:*** Ending the session well is just as important as beginning it well. There is no one right way to do this, but here are some guidelines to consider:

    - Acknowledge everyone for their participation, courage, and willingness to try something new.

    - Ask the group what value they received from the evening and what, specifically, they liked about it.

    - If you've prepared a feedback sheet, invite people to fill it out before leaving.

- Invite people to stay after for informal schmoozing.

- If you've scheduled a second storytelling circle, let people know when and where it will be held, and invite them to help you get the word out. Give them an opportunity to sign up for the next one.

- If you think they would enjoy my book, have some available for purchase or give them the Amazon link.

- Encourage everyone to continue telling their stories outside of the storytelling circle to keep the spirit of storytelling alive.

WHY CREATE A CULTURE OF STORYTELLING?

Unless you've been living in solitary confinement for the past few years, chances are good that you are a member of some kind of organization or community – a gathering of people who have come together in service to a common goal. Whether it's a Fortune 500 company, a non-profit, or a softball team, we are all, whether we know it or not, involved in the process of creating organizational culture – "a collective way of thinking, believing, behaving, and working."

How *conducive* the cultures we create are to the success of our missions is anyone's guess, but what is not a guess is the fact that high-performing organizations exhibit the same kind of mission-enabling qualities: trust, shared vision, collaboration, clear communication, diversity of thought, commitment to learning, freedom of expression, and a sense of belonging.

While there are many ways to enhance these qualities, the most effective and least expensive way is through *storytelling* – a culture-building phenomenon that's been going on since language first began. Simply put, in order for a group of people to accomplish extraordinary goals, they need to know each other at a level far beyond title, role, or resume.

When people tell their stories to each other *and are heard*, magic happens. People bond. Barriers dissolve. Connections are made. Trust increases. Knowledge is transmitted. Wisdom is shared. A common language is birthed. And a deep sense of interdependence is felt. That's why, in days of old, our ancestors stood around the fire and shared their stories with each other. Survival depended on it and so did the emotional well-being of the tribe.

Times have changed since then, as have our methods of communication.

Where once story reigned supreme, now it's technology and all her attention-deficit offspring: texting, Twitter, Instagram, email, Facebook, and drive-by pep talks.

What we've gained in efficiency, we've lost in effectiveness. The spirit of the law has been replaced by the letter. People may be transmitting more, but they are receiving less. We share data, information, and opinions, but not much meaning. And it is *meaning* that people hunger for. It doesn't take a rocket scientist to figure out why employee engagement is down in so many organizations these days. It's because people feel isolated, disconnected, unseen, and unheard.

If you are part of an organization, no matter what it's shape or size, it's time for some meaning making – and that begins by creating engaging opportunities for everyone, from mail room to board room, to share their stories with each other.

WHEN THE LAST STORY HAS BEEN TOLD

"When one is a stranger to oneself, then one is estranged from others, too. If one is out of touch with oneself, then one cannot touch others."

— Anne Morrow Lindbergh

If you've made it this far in the book, there's a good chance you've read most, if not all, of my 38 stories. Thank you. I appreciate your tenacity. What you haven't read, however, are the stories *not* in the book – the stories that didn't make the cut – and there are thousands of them – stories that were too long, too short, too private, too cosmic, too unbelievable, and too hard to write. That's been one of the big revelations I've had while writing this book – how many stories live inside me – and, by extension, how many stories live inside all of us.

But the *real* story, the story *behind* our stories has nothing to do with stories at all.

Let's assume for the moment that you are intrigued by the notion of telling your own stories. Fantastic. Great. That's the reason I wrote the book in this first place. So… you begin thinking about your own moments of truth and start writing them down. The more story titles you write, the more stories you remember – tales from your childhood, travels, work, relationships, quests for meaning, accidents, disappointments, victories, near death experiences, strange lights in the sky, and so on. Let's say you top out at 89 stories. But let's take it one step further. Let's say you actually *write* the stories. But not only write them – you *tell* them too, until every one of your stories has been told. You could, of course, choose to tell your stories again to other people in other ways. You could also turn them into screenplays, novels, songs, sitcoms, iPhone apps, and webinars. But you don't. You feel complete, every story in you having been told. So there you are with no more need to tell a single story (not even the story of why you are no longer telling stories).

Your friends and fans, accustomed to your delightful storytelling, are keenly disappointed, but you say nothing. You say nothing because you have nothing to say. You have no point to make. The words you would normally use to populate your tales have gone south for the winter, vacationing somewhere on a remote island.

Your last story has been told. Though you are fully awake and can see many things happening, you have no need to connect the dots, no need for a plot, characters, conflict, or resolution.

Everything is what it is. You are what you are, breathing slowly, wanting nothing, enjoying the time before the first story was told. You think of telling *that* story, but don't. You let it go. Like the milkweed floating by. Or the leaf…

ABOUT THE AUTHOR

Mitch Ditkoff is the Co-Founder and President of Idea Champions, an innovation consulting and training company dedicated to helping individuals, teams, and entire organizations access the wellspring of their innate creativity in service to accomplishing their ambitious business goals. Since 1987, Mitch has noticed that skillful storytelling is one of the best ways to help his clients tap into their inner wisdom and make innovation real in their lives.

Storytelling at Work is the distillation of his "moments of truth" in the business world. Mitch is also the author of the award-winning book, *Awake at the Wheel*, three books of poetry, The Heart of Innovation blog, and The Heart of the Matter blog. Additionally, he is a regular contributor to The Huffington Post. In 2010 and 2011, he was voted "Best Innovation Blogger in the World" by *Innovation Excellence*, the world's leading innovation portal. Mitch is the husband of peace artist, Evelyne Pouget, and the father of two remarkable human beings, Jesse and Mimi. These days, he divides his time between Woodstock, New York and San Miguel de Allende, Mexico.

LINKS:

Idea Champions:

www.ideachampions.com

Brainstorm Champions:

www.brainstormchampions.com

Heart of Innovation Blog:

www.ideachampions.com/weblogs

Heart of the Matter Blog:

www.ideachampions.com/heart

Huffington Post Articles:

www.huffingtonpost.com/mitch-ditkoff

Awake At The Wheel:

www.awakeatthewheel.info

Full Moon At Sunrise:

available on www.amazon.com

EMAIL: mitch@ideachampions.com

CPSIA information can be obtained
at www.ICGtesting.com
Printed in the USA
FSHW020508221019
63265FS